MARCELO DOS SANTOS

Marcelo Dos Santos is an award-winning Latinx British-Brazilian-Australian writer. *Backstairs Billy* marks Marcelo's West End debut.

Other theatre includes *Feeling Afraid As If Something Terrible is Going to Happen* (Francesca Moody Productions at Summerhall Edinburgh and the Bush Theatre London; winner of the Scotsman Fringe First Award for Excellence in New Writing); *Lionboy* (adaptation for Complicité; UK tour and Broadway); *Trigger Warning* (Camden People's Theatre); *Lovers Walk* (co-writer, Southwark Playhouse); *The End of History* (Soho Theatre/High Hearted Theatre at St Giles in the Fields); *Cheer up this is only the beginning* (co-writer, Liverpool & Everyman Playhouse); *Play Without a Title* (after Lorca; Oxford School of Drama at New Diorama); *Open Plan* (Royal Welsh College of Music and Drama); *New Labour* (RADA, directed by Richard Wilson).

He has been a writer on attachment at the National Theatre, the Bush Theatre, HighTide Festival Theatre and the Royal Court Theatre and was a recipient of an MGC Futures Bursary in 2019.

For screen, Marcelo is developing projects with major companies including Avalon TV, Mam Tor and Drama Republic, and was selected to be a member of the prestigious BBC Drama Room 2019/20.

Other Titles in this Series

Mike Bartlett
THE 47TH
ALBION
BULL
GAME
AN INTERVENTION
KING CHARLES III
MIKE BARTLETT PLAYS: TWO
MRS DELGADO
SCANDALTOWN
SNOWFLAKE
VASSA *after* Gorky
WILD

Chris Bush
THE ASSASSINATION OF KATIE HOPKINS
THE CHANGING ROOM
FAUSTUS: THAT DAMNED WOMAN
HUNGRY
JANE EYRE *after* Brontë
THE LAST NOËL
ROCK/PAPER/SCISSORS
STANDING AT THE SKY'S EDGE
    with Richard Hawley
STEEL

Jez Butterworth
THE FERRYMAN
JERUSALEM
JEZ BUTTERWORTH PLAYS: ONE
JEZ BUTTERWORTH PLAYS: TWO
MOJO
THE NIGHT HERON
PARLOUR SONG
THE RIVER
THE WINTERLING

Caryl Churchill
BLUE HEART
CHURCHILL PLAYS: THREE
CHURCHILL PLAYS: FOUR
CHURCHILL PLAYS: FIVE
CHURCHILL: SHORTS
CLOUD NINE
DING DONG THE WICKED
A DREAM PLAY *after* Strindberg
DRUNK ENOUGH TO SAY I LOVE YOU?
ESCAPED ALONE
FAR AWAY
GLASS. KILL. BLUEBEARD'S FRIENDS.
    IMP.
HERE WE GO
HOTEL
ICECREAM
LIGHT SHINING IN
    BUCKINGHAMSHIRE
LOVE AND INFORMATION
MAD FOREST
A NUMBER
PIGS AND DOGS
SEVEN JEWISH CHILDREN
THE SKRIKER
THIS IS A CHAIR
THYESTES *after* Seneca
TRAPS
WHAT IF IF ONLY

Marcelo Dos Santos
FEELING AFRAID AS IF SOMETHING
    TERRIBLE IS GOING TO HAPPEN
LIONBOY *after* Zizou Corder
NEW LABOUR

Natasha Gordon
NINE NIGHT

Sam Holcroft
COCKROACH
DANCING BEARS
EDGAR & ANNABEL
A MIRROR
PINK
RULES FOR LIVING
THE WARDROBE
WHILE YOU LIE

Lucy Kirkwood
BEAUTY AND THE BEAST
    with Katie Mitchell
BLOODY WIMMIN
THE CHILDREN
CHIMERICA
HEDDA *after* Ibsen
IT FELT EMPTY WHEN THE HEART
    WENT AT FIRST BUT IT IS
    ALRIGHT NOW
LUCY KIRKWOOD PLAYS: ONE
MOSQUITOES
NSFW
RAPTURE
TINDERBOX
THE WELKIN

Suzie Miller
PRIMA FACIE

Winsome Pinnock
LEAVE TAKING
ROCKETS AND BLUE LIGHTS
TAKEN
TITUBA

Jack Thorne
2ND MAY 1997
AFTER LIFE
BUNNY
BURYING YOUR BROTHER IN
    THE PAVEMENT
A CHRISTMAS CAROL *after* Dickens
THE END OF HISTORY...
HOPE
JACK THORNE PLAYS: ONE
JACK THORNE PLAYS: TWO
JUNKYARD
LET THE RIGHT ONE IN
    after John Ajvide Lindqvist
THE MOTIVE AND THE CUE
MYDIDAE
THE SOLID LIFE OF SUGAR WATER
STACY & FANNY AND FAGGOT
WHEN YOU CURE ME
WHEN WINSTON WENT TO WAR WITH
    THE WIRELESS
WOYZECK *after* Büchner

debbie tucker green
BORN BAD
DEBBIE TUCKER GREEN PLAYS: ONE
DIRTY BUTTERFLY
EAR FOR EYE
HANG
NUT
A PROFOUNDLY AFFECTIONATE,
    PASSIONATE DEVOTION TO
    SOMEONE (– *NOUN*)
RANDOM
STONING MARY
TRADE & GENERATIONS
TRUTH AND RECONCILIATION

Phoebe Waller-Bridge
FLEABAG

Marcelo Dos Santos

BACKSTAIRS BILLY

NICK HERN BOOKS
London
www.nickhernbooks.co.uk

A Nick Hern Book

Backstairs Billy first published in Great Britain in 2023 as a paperback original by Nick Hern Books Limited, The Glasshouse, 49a Goldhawk Road, London W12 8QP

Backstairs Billy copyright © 2023 Marcelo Dos Santos

Marcelo Dos Santos has asserted his right to be identified as the author of this work

Cover: Penelope Wilton and Luke Evans; image by AKA/Louise Richardson

Designed and typeset by Nick Hern Books, London
Printed in Great Britain by Mimeo Ltd, Huntingdon, Cambridgeshire PE29 6XX

A CIP catalogue record for this book is available from the British Library

ISBN 978 1 83904 279 9

CAUTION All rights whatsoever in this play are strictly reserved. Requests to reproduce the text in whole or in part should be addressed to the publisher.

Amateur Performing Rights Applications for performance, including readings and excerpts, by amateurs in English should be addressed to the Performing Rights Manager, Nick Hern Books, The Glasshouse, 49a Goldhawk Road, London W12 8QP, *tel* +44 (0)20 8749 4953, *email* rights@nickhernbooks.co.uk, except as follows:

Australia: ORiGiN Theatrical, *email* enquiries@originmusic.com.au, *web* www.origintheatrical.com.au

New Zealand: Play Bureau, 20 Rua Street, Mangapapa, Gisborne, 4010, *tel* +64 21 258 3998, *email* info@playbureau.com

United States of America and Canada: The Agency (London) Ltd, see details below

Professional Performing Rights Applications for performance by professionals in any medium and in any language throughout the world (and amateur and stock performances in the United States of America and Canada) should be addressed to The Agency (London) Ltd, 24 Pottery Lane, Holland Park, London W11 4LZ, *fax* +44 (0)20 7727 9037, *email* info@theagency.co.uk

No performance of any kind may be given unless a licence has been obtained. Applications should be made before rehearsals begin. Publication of this play does not necessarily indicate its availability for amateur performance.

Backstairs Billy was commissioned by MGC, produced by MGC and Sand & Snow Entertainment, and first performed at the Duke of York's Theatre, London, on 7 November 2023 (previews from 27 October). The cast was as follows:

THE QUEEN MOTHER	Penelope Wilton
WILLIAM 'BILLY' TALLON	Luke Evans
ANNABEL MAUDE/ LADY MIFFIE ASTLEBURY	Emily Barber
GWYDION	Iwan Davies
MR KERR	Ian Drysdale
YOUNG BILLY	Ilan Galkoff
IAN	Eloka Ivo
MR HARRINGTON-BAHR/ HUGO MCCOYD	Michael Simkins
MRS HARRINGTON-BAHR/ LADY ADELINE	Nicola Sloane
PALACE STAFF	David Buttle
	Keanu Adolphus Johnson
	Amy Newton
	Georgie Rhys
	Jacob Ethan Tanner
Director	Michael Grandage
Set Designer	Christopher Oram
Costume Designers	Christopher Oram and Tom Rand
Lighting Designer	Ryan Day
Composer and Sound Designer	Adam Cork
Wigs, Hair and Make-up Designer	Carole Hancock
Casting Director	Jacob Sparrow
Associate Director	Sophie Drake

Acknowledgements

Thanks to: Carol McGowan, Rhys Warrington, Kenny Emson, Satya Bhabha, Dr Laura Schwartz, Simon Blakey and Seán Butler at The Agency, as well as all at Nick Hern Books. And biggest thank-you of all to Michael Grandage and Nick Frankfort for commissioning and staging this production and all the work the Michael Grandage Company does to support theatre artists through the MGC Futures Bursary.

M.D.S.

Characters

WILLIAM (BILLY) TALLON
THE QUEEN MOTHER
GWYDION
IAN
MR KERR
ANNABEL MAUDE
MRS HARRINGTON-BAHR
MR HARRINGTON-BAHR
LADY MIFFIE ASTLEBURY
HUGO McCOYD
LADY ADELINE
YOUNG BILLY

Additional FOOTMEN, MAIDS

Setting

Clarence House, London, 1979 and 1952.

This play is a fictitious work based in part on real people. Characters and incidents have been invented by the author for dramatic and comedic purposes.

This text went to press before the end of rehearsals and so may differ slightly from the play as performed.

Scene One

April, 1979. The Garden Room of Clarence House.

At the centre of the room is a double door leading to a hallway which can be glimpsed when the doors are opened. There are also doors either side of the room.

It is exactly as you expect the Queen Mother's house: pinks, pastels, chintz. It's glorious and defiantly dated, even for the time.

There are a series of small tables, plinths for vases, and sideboards lining the walls. In the centre is a giant rose-coloured rug and in the centre of that, a sofa and a few small armchairs.

The central door opens. We expect a person, instead three corgis enter the room.

A beat as they sniff around.

Enter BILLY *(forty-four, tall, a sweep of dyed-black hair, immaculate morning suit) followed by a line of* MAIDS *and* FOOTMEN, *including* GWYDION *(mid-twenties) carrying flowers in vases all in different shades of pink: camellias, Albertine roses, sweet peas.*

The dogs bark. BILLY *looks at the corgis and they run offstage.*

BILLY *swiftly but carefully walks along the edge of the carpet to one end of the room. The* SERVANTS *form a line, awaiting his orders.*

He carefully appraises the flower arrangements.

BILLY. Rosewood.

One moves towards a rosewood table, keeping to the side of the rug.

Occasional.

Another SERVANT *peels off towards the occasional table.*

Sideboard.

Another SERVANT *goes towards a sideboard.*

BILLY *indicates a* SERVANT *with two quite similar flowers in their hands.*

Plinth. Plinth.

The SERVANT *puts them on the plinths.*

Pier.

A fifth SERVANT *goes outside into the corridor.*

They place the vases in the appointed position in sync, they look up for his approval.

Rosewood occasional. Occasional rosewood.

They criss-cross, place and wait for his approval.

He keeps them in suspense.

He walks to each, perhaps turns the vase.

Sideboard, occasional, occasional, pier.

They start moving.

(*Louder.*) Pier?

The SERVANT *in the corridor returns with the flowers.*

Sideboard.

He goes to the sideboard.

No. Absolutely not. Sideboard?

GWYDION. Yes, sir?

BILLY. Rosewood. Rosewood sideboard.

They criss-cross and then, in sync, place down the vases.

Plinth?

BILLY *considers the flowers and their placement.*

Plinth.

He gestures for the two vases on the plinth to be swapped.

The two vases on the plinths are swapped but are essentially identical.

Very good. There it is.

He nods his head; the remaining staff take this as a cue, except for GWYDION *who seems unsure of his exit and goes to cross the carpet.*

You.

GWYDION. Sir?

BILLY. Stop.

Caught, GWYDION *stops in his tracks.*

What are you doing?

GWYDION. The guests…

BILLY. The edge.

GWYDION. Sir?

BILLY. Step to the edge.

GWYDION *hesitates.*

The edge of the carpet. The very edge.

GWYDION. Like this?

GWYDION *steps away from the centre of the carpet.*

BILLY. Yes, like that. Well done, dearie. Now come here.

GWYDION *moves towards him.*

No, along the edge. The centre of the carpet is reserved for the family. You must always, always walk on the edge.

GWYDION *starts the L-shaped walk along the edge of the carpet to reach* BILLY. *He is self-conscious, hesitant.*

A little quicker now. Quicker, quicker, dear God, boy, who have you got up there?

He shuffles along faster. He reaches BILLY.

Oh, you made it, well done.

GWYDION. Thank you, sir.

BILLY. Now, what is it?

GWYDION. The guests are waiting.

BILLY. Well, I should hope so.

GWYDION. Should we bring them in?

BILLY. *We* will do nothing. *I* will bring them from the Lancaster Room at three p.m., is it three p.m.?

GWYDION. No, sir.

BILLY. It is three p.m. in exactly… twelve minutes. And her majesty will be precisely fifteen minutes late. She is fond of an entrance.

GWYDION. Yes, sir.

BILLY. You're new.

GWYDION. Yes, sir.

BILLY. Name?

GWYDION. Gwydion, sir.

BILLY. Did Reg hire you?

GWYDION. Yes. Sir. My friend Gary, sir. Gary Lewis, he used to work here, sir. He was a junior footman, sir, and he said I should speak to –

BILLY. Lewis? Oh, yes. (*Looks at* GWYDION *afresh.*) Yes… I remember Gary. Northern?

GWYDION. Yes.

BILLY. Tall?

GWYDION. Yes.

BILLY. Chipped tooth?

GWYDION. Yes.

BILLY. Stupendously hung?

GWYDION. Yes.

Beat.

I mean –

BILLY. It wasn't a question. Everybody knows Gary…

GWYDION. Yes, sir.

A moment of connection between the two men.

BILLY. Works at a pub in Soho now, yes?

GWYDION. The Duncan, yes.

BILLY. The Duncan indeed. And what did Gary tell you about us?

GWYDION. He said it was interesting.

BILLY. How kind of him. What else?

GWYDION. That he learnt a lot.

BILLY. Now I know you're lying. He told you the address and that food and board's included.

GWYDION. Yes, sir, he did mention that.

BILLY. Well, it is quite the postcode, but the food is inedible and it's not all bedhopping. I hope he told you that too.

GWYDION. Yes, sir.

BILLY. We shall see. Stand up.

GWYDION. Sir?

BILLY. Stand up. Up up up up up. Head on a string. There. Maintain that. As a footman you will need to be able to stand and stand for hours on end; to be utterly present without ever distracting. To be always ready without appearing to want. It is hard, hard work and there can be no mistakes.

GWYDION. Yes, sir.

BILLY. Especially today. I'm afraid word has reached us that her majesty has had a trying morning.

GWYDION. Is she ill?

BILLY. Of course not. Her majesty is never ill. She is only very occasionally tired. This morning has been *trying*.

GWYDION. Because of the man from the bank?

BILLY. Who told you that?

GWYDION. No one, sir.

BILLY. That kind of talk is completely unacceptable.

GWYDION. Sorry, sir.

BILLY. I will not tolerate gossip inside of these walls and outside of these walls it's a criminal offence, is that clear?

GWYDION. Yes, sir. I'm sorry, sir.

BILLY. Discretion is absolutely essential.

He looks around.

For us all. You're very lucky it was only me who heard.

GWYDION. Thank you, sir.

BILLY. Remember, it is not for us to speculate on the whys of anything. Her majesty is hugely busy and has meetings with all sorts of advisers, all of the time, financial and otherwise. The details do not concern us. All that matters to us, is knowing what she wants. If you are serious about being a footman, that is the most important thing to master. We are there to give her what she wants before she even knows what she wants. And what she tends to want after that sort of meeting, which tends to be… 'trying', is for everything to run like clockwork. It's not too much to ask, is it?

GWDYION. No, sir.

BILLY. She has after all given so much for this country.

GWYDION. Yes, sir. The war, sir.

BILLY. Up, up, up.

GWYDION *raises his head.*

BILLY *considers him.*

And do you like it so far?

GWYDION. What, sir?

BILLY. Service? Clarence House?

GWYDION. Very much so, sir.

BILLY. Why?

GWYDION. I like knowing what I'm doing.

BILLY. Which is amusing, because you don't.

GWYDION. Yes, sir. I know, sir. But I like that there is a proper way of doing things.

BILLY *takes this in, then moves away.*

BILLY. Yes, you're quite good-looking.

GWYDION. Thank you, sir.

BILLY. From certain angles. (*Turning back.*) That one.

GWYDION. Sir?

BILLY. But not that one. There.

GWYDION *freezes.*

Stay like that, indefinitely if possible. You stand beside priceless works of art, you open doors older than modern democracy, you walk the same halls as ancient princes, it's only right, it's only proper that you have some sort of bearing, don't you think? It's not like we ask for O levels.

GWYDION. I have O levels.

BILLY (*camping it up*). Well, hark at her; I don't, dearie.

GWYDION. I'm sorry, sir.

BILLY. Don't be sorry, I'm not. Can't see the point myself.

Beat.

But I take it you don't object?

GWYDION. What's that, sir?

BILLY. I take it you don't entirely object to being... an ornament?

GWYDION. No, sir...

A frisson.

BILLY. Very good. And it appears you *can* stand which knowing Gary Lewis is something of a miracle. Knowing Gary, it's a wonder you can walk.

GWYDION. Where there's a will there's a way, sir.

BILLY *laughs*.

BILLY. That's the spirit.

MR KERR (*early fifties, an equerry*) *enters*.

KERR. Billy?

An awkward formality asserts itself.

BILLY (*turning to* KERR). Mr Kerr, how can I help?

KERR. Is everything in place?

BILLY. Naturally.

KERR *looks at* GWYDION.

KERR. Who are you?

BILLY. Mr Kerr, this is Gwydion.

KERR. Are you new? What's he doing here? Is he new?

BILLY. He is. He's Welsh.

KERR. Was I informed?

BILLY. About the Welsh? I'd like to think we're in a constant state of readiness.

KERR. I need to be informed, William, when you are taking on new staff.

BILLY (*to* GWYDION). Wait outside.

GWYDION *exits.*

BILLY *goes to the drinks cabinet. He starts taking out various bottles and properly setting up the drinks.*

KERR. Well, Billy.

BILLY. Mr Kerr?

KERR. Her majesty is very much looking forward to the reception for this afternoon.

BILLY. That is my understanding.

KERR. And keen for all to go well.

BILLY. Well, yes, naturally… Or do you mean particularly after this morning? This morning was quite the inconvenience.

KERR (*warning*). Billy.

BILLY (*innocent*). Yes, Mr Kerr?

KERR. We are never inconvenienced.

BILLY *bows gravely, delicately balancing the formal with the ironic.*

BILLY. I speak, of course, of her majesty's inconvenience, which if I understand my duties correctly is to at the very least ameliorate, if not entirely banish from the face of the earth.

KERR *sighs.*

But why her majesty has to submit herself to scrutiny of that little man from Coutts I'll never know.

KERR. And it is not for you to know.

Beat.

BILLY. Is that all, Mr Kerr?

KERR. Actually, there is a certain member of the WI attending the reception.

BILLY. Mrs Harrington-Bahr.

KERR. Mr and Mrs Harrington-Bahr do not drink.

BILLY. Not even champagne?

KERR. Not even champagne.

BILLY. Not even for her majesty? How terribly unpatriotic. Oh well, desperately sad news but we shall overcome. I will make sure we have the finest PG Tips at the ready and I will send out for... a mug?

KERR. And I would request most strongly that the 'enjoyment' generally could be contained / somewhat moving forward.

BILLY. Curtailed?

KERR. Not curtailed, just contained.

BILLY. In what? Tupperware? I'm sure I can find some staff leftovers to reheat if you think that would be appropriate for the country's most popular person, former Queen Consort and the last Empress of India.

KERR (*sharp*). That's enough, Billy. Don't forget you have additional responsibilities now you are Page of the Backstairs.

BILLY. I am well aware of that and my commitment to her majesty is total.

KERR. Not just to her majesty.

BILLY. I'm sorry, Mr Kerr, I'm not sure what that means.

KERR. You have a responsibility to the Crown.

BILLY. Naturally.

KERR. And the Crown's purse.

BILLY (*teasing*). Mr Kerr, however can you doubt my passion for purses?

KERR. Billy, you encourage her.

BILLY. Her majesty is a queen. I serve her. I am merely a servant.

KERR. If only you believed that... Do you have any idea what's going on out there, Billy?

SCENE ONE 19

BILLY. Where? The Mall? Traffic I expect. Frightful at this hour.

KERR. The country is on its knees.

BILLY. There are worse places to be. I hear we have a hung parliament.

KERR. I am being serious, Billy. The palace is watching us closely. It is concerned by a lack of caution.

BILLY. Caution?

KERR. Yes, a lack of caution in all things. Things are at a delicate pass, politically, financially. The pressure is enormous.

BILLY. Not everyone can cope with pressure, of course. Would you like to sit down?

KERR. What? No, of course not. I speak about the pressure on all of us.

BILLY. The only pressure I feel, Mr Kerr, is the pressure to be the best servant I can to her majesty.

KERR. If you are to be Page –

BILLY. There is no 'if'. I am Page of the Backstairs now, Mr Kerr.

KERR. I had hoped we could move beyond this and work together.

BILLY. Do we not?

KERR. That is entirely up to you.

BILLY does not respond. GWYDION enters.

GWYDION. Sorry, sir, it's three p.m.

BILLY. If you'll excuse me, Mr Kerr.

KERR reluctantly exits. BILLY goes to the drinks cabinet and takes a swig from a tumbler.

Gwydion? No, actually, that won't do, Gwydion's far too long. Daffodil? Daff! There it is. Daff?

GWYDION. Yes, sir?

BILLY. This afternoon will be a challenge. We are not exactly blessed with an ideal cast of players and they will be terribly nervous. Even interesting people, and these will not be interesting people, find themselves tongue-tied and stupid around her majesty. Kerr has dug up a couple of Home Counties cadavers called Mr and Mrs Harrington-Bahr because he wishes to personally torment me. They are 'teetotallers', can you imagine? Of course, I have a fix for that.

GWYDION. A fix, sir?

BILLY. Cordial.

GWYDION. Sir?

BILLY. With, a dash of… panache.

Holds up a bottle of something.

GWYDION. But they don't drink.

BILLY (*enjoying it*). Do I shock you, Daff?

GWYDION (*unsure*). No, sir.

BILLY. I'll have to try harder. Her majesty deserves the best from her guests and we are here to serve her majesty, not Mr and Mrs Harrington-Bahr. Thank. God. Fortunately, their presence is slightly offset by the delightful Annabel Maude, do you know her? Do you watch her? Terribly fun. She will be no trouble at all. Follow my lead in all things. Head up. Arse in. Goes against all one's natural instincts but there it is. We're going over the top.

He walks perfectly along the edge of the carpet, followed by GWYDION, *and they exit.*

A corgi runs through the room and exits.

Moments later, BILLY *strides in through the central doors followed by* GWYDION.

Please do come in.

SCENE ONE 21

A little clutch of nervous, overdressed guests inch forward.
ANNABEL *(actress, late twenties);* MR HARRINGTON-BAHR *(formal, mid-sixties, a bit deaf);* MRS HARRINGTON-BAHR *(mid-sixties, formidable).*

Please *do* come in. We don't bite. Or at least very rarely. And the dogs hardly at all.

A too-loud laugh from ANNABEL.

They move forward but hover near the door, unsure who is around the corner.

Her majesty will be with us shortly.

Visible relief from ANNABEL *that she's not there yet.*

They look around the space.

ANNABEL. Bloody hell, Billy.

BILLY. Language, darling.

ANNABEL. What did I say? Did I swear? I don't know I'm doing it half the time. You must stop me, Billy.

MRS BAHR. Do you two know each other?

ANNABEL. Oh Billy knows everyone.

BILLY. Hardly.

ANNABEL. And everyone knows Billy.

MRS BAHR. Well, I don't know him.

BILLY. No.

Beat as ANNABEL *looks about the room.*

ANNABEL. God, this place is something, isn't it?

BILLY. We try our best.

ANNABEL. The curtains.

BILLY. Damask, silk.

ANNABEL. And the flowers. All the flowers. What are these ones called?

BILLY. Roses.

ANNABEL (*laughing*). Oh God, really? What an idiot I am, but I really am useless at living things. Flowers, children –

MRS BAHR. Pink Albertines?

BILLY. That's correct, Mrs Harrington-Bahr. Pink Albertine roses. You have an excellent eye.

MRS BAHR (*pointing to the other bunch*). Camellias.

BILLY. Camellias that's right.

MRS BAHR. Sweet peas.

ANNABEL (*to* BILLY, *under her breath*). It's not a competition, duckie…

MR BAHR. Sweet pea is it?

BILLY. One of her majesty's favourites.

MRS BAHR. We grow the Elizabeth of Glamis in our garden at home. (*To* BILLY.) That is her majesty's rose.

BILLY. I am aware. (*Deeply ironic*.) Her majesty will be thrilled.

ANNABEL. And the ceilings are simply. What are they? What's the word?

BILLY. Tall?

ANNABEL *laughs*.

ANNABEL. I'm not a complete idiot, Billy. They are grand. That's the word. Terribly grand.

MR BAHR. John Nash is it? The architect.

BILLY. Yes and no. The house suffered dreadfully during the war and it was quite altered even before then. Tragically nothing really remains of the original John Nash entrance which was quite the occasion. He did Brighton Pavilion, so porticos and whatnot. Hard to imagine but there it is. Hitler really does have a lot to answer for.

MR BAHR. The most dangerous woman in Europe that's what Hitler called her.

BILLY. Hitler was of course correct. (*To the group, stern.*) However, when you are introduced you will call her 'your majesty' and thereafter 'ma'am'. You may nod or curtsy. Do not address her directly. Do not ask her questions. Do not eat before she does. Do not leave the room before she does.

MR BAHR (*offended but chastened*). Of course.

ANNABEL. What if you need to…?

BILLY. You do not need to.

ANNABEL. I'm scared, are you scared?

BILLY. Don't be scared. Her majesty adores company. The rules are in place for your benefit so as to avoid embarrassment or confusion.

ANNABEL. I feel really quite hysterical. (*To* MRS HARRINGTON-BAHR.) Do you feel hysterical?

MRS BAHR. No.

BILLY. Annabel, would you like a drink?

ANNABEL. God, yes.

BILLY. What would you like?

ANNABEL. Oh, you know me, as long as it's wet.

He pours some champagne into ANNABEL*'s glass.*

BILLY. Sherry, Mrs Harrington-Bahr?

MRS BAHR. No, thank you. Mr Harrington-Bahr and I do not drink.

BILLY. But you'll have champagne?

MRS BAHR. We are teetotal.

BILLY. Mr Harrington-Bahr though surely?

MRS BAHR. Won't touch a drop. Not since the war.

MR BAHR. What's that?

MRS BAHR. Alcohol, dear.

MR BAHR. Never touch the stuff. Not since the war.

BILLY. I'm so sorry, I wasn't informed.

MRS BAHR. I understood this to be tea.

BILLY. Of course. Let me find you something more suitable.

BILLY *goes towards the drinks cabinet, he gives* GWYDION *the eye to follow him.*

MRS BAHR (*to* ANNABEL). So I understand you are an actress?

MR BAHR. Is she what?

MRS BAHR. An actress.

MR BAHR. Is she?

MRS BAHR. Are you? We don't recognise you, do we?

MR BAHR. What?

MRS BAHR. We don't recognise her.

MR BAHR. Who?

MRS BAHR. The actress. Not that we would. (*To* ANNABEL.) We don't really go to the theatre. Not quite sure we understand it.

ANNABEL. Oh well.

MRS BAHR. Perhaps you can explain.

ANNABEL. Theatre?

MRS BAHR. Yes, perhaps you can explain it?

Beat.

ANNABEL. Gosh. Not really. It doesn't really make sense if you think about it too much.

MRS BAHR. And we don't watch TV, you see. We only have a set because our Nigel insisted. He works in aviation, of course.

ANNABEL. Of course.

MRS BAHR. We have it on for the Queen's Speech and in case of war but other than that we don't see the point.

BILLY *comes over with two tumblers of fizzy drink on a tray. He hands them to the* HARRINGTON-BAHRS.

What is it?

BILLY. I believe it is what they call a soft drink. I myself have never tried one.

They drink cautiously.

A moment of suspense.

MRS BAHR. What does it taste of? It reminds me of something.

BILLY. Spring, Mrs Harrington-Bahr. It tastes of spring.

MR BAHR. I like it.

BILLY. Excellent. (*In order to distract.*) More champagne, Annabel darling?

He gestures to GWYDION *to fill the glass.*

ANNABEL. Rather.

BILLY. Gwydion –

GWYDION *pours champagne.*

ANNABEL (*to* GWYDION). Oh you're a pretty one, aren't you?

BILLY. Careful, Annabel.

ANNABEL. Don't worry, Billy, you're still the fairest of them all.

BILLY. Annabel is the star of one of her majesty's favourite TV shows.

MRS BAHR. Is that right?

ANNABEL. So I'm told.

She downs her drink.

BILLY. She watches it, dare I say, religiously.

MRS BAHR. *Songs of Praise*, of course and Royal Events, of course, the Silver Jubilee of course and in case of war but other than that nothing.

BILLY. It is a very popular comedy.

MRS BAHR. A comedy?

ANNABEL. A sitcom. A situation comedy…

MRS BAHR. And it is her majesty's favourite?

BILLY *bows his head in acknowledgement.*

Well, we shall have to watch.

ANNABEL. I really wouldn't bother, it's awful tosh.

BILLY. Annabel!

ANNABEL. Is that awful of me? Yes, that's dreadful I mustn't say that in front of her. That's exactly the kind of thing that would come out of my mouth. Or worse. Shit, what if I say shit?

Gasps.

Gosh, this has gone straight to my head.

BILLY *claps.*

A FOOTMAN *swoops in with a platter of gold boxes with white or pink bows.*

What's this?! Is it Christmas?

MR BAHR. Is it?

MRS BAHR. No, dear, it's April.

BILLY. These are not gifts; these are curios, 'objets' if you like, drawn from the Royal Archives. I thought they might be of interest to you, and perhaps might serve as interesting talking points with her majesty later.

ANNABEL. Oh God, what was it again I was supposed to say? 'Mam' or 'maahm'?

She takes a box or is given one by BILLY *and starts unwrapping it.*

MR BAHR. 'Mam' as in Spam.

MRS BAHR. Is there food, Mr Tallon? I'm suddenly feeling a little faint.

BILLY. Once her majesty has arrived. Have a little more cordial.

He pours more cordial into the HARRINGTON-BAHRS' *tumblers from a decanter.*

ANNABEL (*opening the box and showing an old theatre programme*). Oh it's a darling old theatre programme.

BILLY. It is signed by Sir Noël Coward himself to her majesty.

ANNABEL. Is it? Gosh, September 1930. What does it say? I can't make it out.

BILLY. Perhaps you can ask her majesty?

ANNABEL. Really no?

MR BAHR. What's this then?

BILLY. Mittens.

MRS BAHR. Oh?

BILLY. Knitted by her majesty during the war for our boys on the front.

MRS BAHR. Heavens. No?

BILLY. Heavens, yes.

MRS BAHR. Knitted by her very hands?

BILLY. By her very hands.

MRS HARRINGTON-BAHR *lifts the gloves like a holy relic towards the lights.*

MRS BAHR. A waffle stitch. (*Nodding*.) But of course.

MR BAHR. Of course.

ANNABEL. What else should we talk to her about though, Billy? Small talk? That's right, isn't it?

BILLY. Not at all, duckie. Her majesty is terribly curious about people. Please don't be afraid to be yourselves.

MRS BAHR. Of course.

BILLY. Unless you happen to be terribly boring, in which case I would ask that you make an effort.

ANNABEL. What does she find boring?

BILLY. She is always interested, always curious about everything, but I would avoid politics at all costs.

ANNABEL. Oh dear, I voted for Labour last time. Will she hold that against me?

BILLY. Only if you do it again.

ANNABEL. God, no. I'm voting for this Thatcher creature. There's something terribly repertory about her which I find very comforting. Although everyone says her politics are awful.

MR BAHR. Well, something needs to be done about the mess out there. These people, these strikes. That Scargill man.

BILLY. No well, it's exactly this we want to avoid. A top-up, Mr Harrington-Bahr.

The doors open and the corgis run in, followed by the QUEEN MOTHER (QM). *She smiles beatifically at everyone without really attaching her gaze.*

BILLY *bows.*

Everyone bows or curtsies with varying degrees of success.

May I introduce Ms Annabel Maude, ma'am.

QM. No but of course I recognise Ms Maude.

She moves towards ANNABEL.

We love your programme, don't we, Billy?

BILLY. We do, ma'am.

QM. It does make us laugh, even though I supposed we shouldn't because it is terribly rude. And I hear you were in that marvellous Coward. Quite sold out. I couldn't even get tickets. Billy went of course. I don't know how he does it. Was she wonderful?

BILLY. Wonderful.

QM. Wonderful. Noël was a dear friend. Terribly naughty. Did you ever get to meet him?

ANNABEL *is silent.*

(*To* BILLY.) Is there something wrong with her?

BILLY. Annabel dear?

ANNABEL. I'm sorry, your majesty, I've completely forgotten how to speak.

QM. Oh dear. Something of an emergency for an actress, I imagine. Unless you're a mime I suppose, but I do find them rather silly. Billy, what was the name of that mime?

BILLY. Marcel Marceau, ma'am.

QM. Marcel Marceau. Rather chatty as it turned out. French, you know?

BILLY. And this is Mr and Mrs Harrington-Bahr, ma'am.

MRS HARRINGTON-BAHR *practically genuflects.*

QM. Goodness.

She looks to BILLY, *who struggles to conceal his disdain.*

Just as well Billy cleaned the carpet this morning. And where have you come from today, Mrs Harrington-Bahr?

MRS BAHR. Hertfordshire, your majesty.

QM. Oh, very good.

MRS BAHR. The train, I'm afraid, was late.

QM. Is that right? Well, I shall have to have a word.

MRS BAHR. Oh no, that is not necessary, your majesty, we would have walked.

QM. Yes? Well. Yes. Very good. And Mr Harrington-Bahr? Are you well?

MR HARRINGTON-BAHR*'s head is still bowing, unable to meet her gaze.*

MR BAHR. On behalf of the St Ippolytus Rotary Club.

MRS BAHR. And the St Ippolytus Women's Institute.

MR BAHR. We would like to thank you for your many years of tireless and unparalleled service to the Royal County of Hertfordshire.

QM. Very good.

Beat.

Just Hertfordshire?

MR BAHR. Ma'am?

QM. My service?

MRS BAHR. And to the United Kingdom.

QM. Oh good. I worried for a moment Hertfordshire was lost like India or Kenya and someone forgot to tell me.

MR BAHR. Never, your majesty.

QM. No, it very well could happen. We are quite out of the way here in our funny little house. Quite apart from the dizzying whirl of world events. Not that we mind that, do we, Billy?

BILLY. No, ma'am.

QM. It is a funny sort of court, you see, but it is ours. Well, we are always glad to be of service, Mr and Mrs Harrington-Bahr, to the democratic republic of Hertfordshire.

MR *and* MRS HARRINGTON-BAHR *bow too deeply again and* MR HARRINGTON-BAHR *stumbles slightly. Perhaps burps?*

ANNABEL. Oops.

MRS BAHR. Apologies, your majesty.

QM. Not at all. Perhaps you would like some water? I'm not sure where it's kept but I expect Billy could bore a well.

MR BAHR. We have cordial, ma'am.

QM. I see. That's rather dispiriting, isn't it?

MRS BAHR. It is actually delicious, ma'am.

QM. Oh good.

MRS BAHR. With a very unusual flavour.

QM. Oh really? How wonderful.

FOOTMEN and MAIDS enter with canapés and swirl around them.

BILLY takes the half-empty decanter back to the drinks trolley, followed by GWYDION.

ANNABEL. Oh gosh. How lovely.

QM. Yes do eat up. I hear the 'grub' is excellent.

GWYDION – and us – see BILLY pouring gallons of vodka into the juice drink.

GWYDION. No more, sir, surely?

BILLY. Why ever not?

GWYDION. They'll be blotto. That's too much, sir.

BILLY. No. Such. Thing.

A booming laugh from MR HARRINGTON-BAHR. The SERVANTS swirl as BILLY moves towards the guests with the drinks under the following.

QM (*to* ANNABEL). Now, Miss Maude, does it take a terribly long time to film your show?

ANNABEL. Not really, ma'am. Only if we make mistakes.

QM. And do you make a lot of mistakes?

ANNABEL. All the time.

QM. Oh good. I always think the mistakes are the funniest bits.

ANNABEL. Tell that to my director.

As BILLY *reaches them, he presents the tray.*

BILLY. Mr and Mrs Harrington-Bahr? More cordial.

QM. Billy, do we know the director of Annabel's show?

BILLY. No, ma'am.

QM. Do we want to know the director?

BILLY. No, ma'am.

QM. Good, apparently, he's terribly firm with Miss Maude just because she makes mistakes. No, I adore the accidental. I would happily watch an entire show where people just walk into things. And accents! I do enjoy voices. Do you do voices, Annabel? I'm sure you do voices. Do voices.

ANNABEL. I can do a 'wee bit of Scots'.

QM (*not impressed*). Oh I see.

ANNABEL. And Bir-mingham, ma'am.

QM. Billy knows all about that one.

BILLY. Yes, ma'am. Coventry but equally benighted.

QM. Barely comprehensible when he first joined service. And now he's posher than all of us put together.

BILLY (*posher than ever*). Oh my, the very thought. But her majesty has yet to meet young Gwydion here. He is Welsh.

QM. Oh yes? Do some of that.

GWYDION (*startled*). Ma'am?

BILLY. Go on, boy.

GWYDION *hesitates then sings –*

SCENE ONE

GWYDION.
>Calon lân yn llawn daioni,
>Tecach yw na'r lili dlos,
>Dim ond calon lân all ganu
>Canu'r dydd a chanu'r nos.

QM. Good heavens, what was that?

GWYDION. 'Calon Lân', ma'am. It's a Welsh hymn.

QM. How lovely. But I rather meant the accent. Do the accent, we love the accent.

GWYDION. People always say I don't have much of an accent, ma'am.

QM (*disappointed*). Oh.

GWDYION (*putting it on*). But it's really lovely to be here, ma'am, even though I am so far away from my home... in the Valleys.

QM. Yes, there, you see. Perhaps you can do another song for us later. Something stirring. Do you do voices, Mrs Harrington-Bahr?

MRS BAHR. Oh. Well, I uhm.

QM. No, well, not everyone can, you see.

MR BAHR. Howdy.

Everyone turns to look.

QM. What's that?

MR BAHR. Howdy... partner.

QM. What was that, Mr Harrington-Bahr?

MRS BAHR. Neville?

MR BAHR. I said, howdy partner...

MRS BAHR. I'm so sorry, your majesty, I don't know what he's doing.

QM. I think he's trying to communicate. Is that your American?

MR BAHR. Yes, ma'am. I'm sorry, I don't know what came over me.

QM. No, it's very good. Can you do a bit more?

MR BAHR (*he thinks about it*). No, ma'am.

QM. That's a shame. Well, perhaps that's the end of that.

MRS BAHR. I can do Indian.

The younger staff look to each other, not quite believing what they're seeing.

Champagne popping sound.

Lights down.

Scene Two

Lights up. Same location. An hour later. The guests have left but QM *and* BILLY *are still there, poised to do a post-party post-mortem.*

QM. Well…

BILLY. Well.

Don't blame me. The Harrington-Bores came from Kerr.

QM. Harrington-Bores, Billy?

BILLY. Apologies, ma'am, I misspoke.

QM. They perked up though, didn't they?

BILLY. They did indeed.

QM. Quite remarkably so. And the little girl was very entertaining. We'll have her again.

BILLY. Yes, ma'am, very good, ma'am.

QM. And this new footman?

SCENE TWO 35

BILLY. Gwydion?

QM. The very spit of you at that age.

BILLY. Perhaps. We will see if he has what it takes.

QM. Who do we have tonight?

BILLY. A professor of physics.

QM. Oh dear.

BILLY. The director of the Royal Opera House.

QM. Fine, as long as we don't have to talk about opera.

BILLY. The French cultural attaché.

QM. As long as we don't have to talk about culture. Or France.

BILLY. And John Curry; the ice-dancer.

QM. How nice. One for you, Billy.

BILLY. Yes, ma'am.

QM. Any more?

BILLY. Well, the list was longer but I will have to check with Mr Kerr.

QM. Kerr?

BILLY. Yes, ma'am. He said something about the need to contain events somewhat?

QM. Contain? Contain in what? I don't understand.

BILLY. I'm afraid I don't either, ma'am. Perhaps I misunderstood but he seemed to imply we may want to contain hospitality somewhat in the light of… fiscal events.

QM. Well, Mr Kerr isn't the one being forced to talk about physics. Physics!

BILLY. Yes, ma'am. I'm sure it's a misunderstanding.

QM. Yes, I'm sure it is.

BILLY. Shall I speak to Mr Kerr again?

QM. Oh I don't think that's necessary, just make sure we always have what we need. You're so clever at that.

BILLY. Yes, ma'am, of course, ma'am.

QM. Put on a record, Billy.

He goes to the record player and puts on a record – a waltz, something jazzier?

He brings forward some magazines for her to choose from. She points at one and he brings it to her even though it's within reaching distance. The routine is well-practised.

She leafs through the magazine without really absorbing it.

BILLY *stands to one side, waiting.*

Any messages from the family?

BILLY. Not that I'm aware of.

QM. Princess Margaret?

BILLY. No, ma'am.

QM *nods to herself. There is a sadness.*

QM. Billy?

BILLY. Ma'am.

QM. When did everyone become so obsessed with money?

BILLY. I have no idea, ma'am.

QM. I don't think it's healthy.

BILLY. Yes I shouldn't think so, ma'am.

QM. It's a sickness in a way. It can eat away at you.

BILLY. Yes, ma'am.

QM. Of course, I understand the times. Difficult times. Economic times.

Silence.

As if there have never been difficult economic times before. As if there had never been riots before. Did you read about that one? Everyone acting appalled. Each generation thinking they invented something terribly new, when in fact, they are just seeing it for the first time. But one worries of course. Although what is the use of that?

BILLY. Very little, ma'am, I'm sure.

QM. I was once talking to a nice young man, were you there, you were there – we were in Essex somewhere – and it was just after the Cuban Missile Crisis and when someone asked if he was worried, he said 'About wot?' He didn't know anything about it and I thought that was rather wise. What is to be gained? Oh to be able not to worry, for once.

BILLY. Quite so, ma'am.

BILLY hands her a chocolate box.

QM. Jolly good.

She takes one.

And then another.

She sighs.

No, it's no good, I'm out of sorts.

BILLY. Is her majesty in pain?

QM. Of course not. Why would I be in pain? It's just the inconvenience. What's the point of being in town if you can't see anyone? If you have to waste your time poring over account books when you pay people, seemingly far too much, to do just that and it's still not enough. Contained, you say?

BILLY inclines his head.

In what? Tupperware?

BILLY nods his agreement.

And to think we used to command an empire.

She catches herself.

Well yes, I suppose we shall, shall we?

BILLY. Ma'am?

QM. Dance.

> BILLY *doesn't know how to respond.*
>
> Did I not say that aloud?

BILLY. You did, ma'am.

QM. I don't think I did. I thought it but I didn't say it out loud. I'll not have you saying I'm senile.

BILLY. Yes, ma'am.

QM. Let's dance then, shall we?

> *She stands up.*
>
> *He moves towards her. She presents her hand. He takes it and gently they assume a ballroom hold.*
>
> Up, up, up. Head on a string.

BILLY. Yes, ma'am.

> *They dance for a few moments. She is remarkably light on her feet.*
>
> *A knock on the door. We see* KERR *hovering and watching them. There is a strange wistfulness to his look.*
>
> *They notice him and stop dancing.* BILLY *moves to the record player.*

QM. Yes, Mr Kerr?

KERR. Your majesty. May we speak?

QM. Of course.

> KERR *looks to* BILLY. QM *follows his eyeline, nods her head, dismissing* BILLY.
>
> BILLY *bows and exits.*

KERR. I trust your majesty had a pleasant afternoon.

QM (*sighing*). Well, we are quite used to rationing from the war of course.

SCENE TWO 39

KERR. Ma'am?

QM. It was very nice event, thank you, Mr Kerr. If somewhat spartan.

KERR. I am surprised, ma'am.

QM. As am I.

KERR. The Harrington-Bahrs, ma'am –

QM. I think it's pronounced Harrington-Bore.

KERR. Is that right, ma'am?

QM. Yes, they told me themselves. Most unfortunate name for such riveting conversationalists.

KERR. The Harrington-Bores, ma'am, they required assistance.

QM. Oh dear. Whatever is the matter?

KERR. That is what I am trying to ascertain, but they appear to be inebriated.

QM. That can't be right, they were drinking cordial all afternoon.

KERR. Yes, ma'am, that is the mystery.

QM. Are you quite sure? They mentioned walking here, perhaps they were just tired? It's a long walk from St Ippolytus.

KERR. Quite sure. They have been quite sick.

QM. Oh dear.

KERR. Demonstrably sick.

QM. Oh dear, do you mean – ?

KERR. Yes, ma'am.

QM. Where?

KERR. In an ottoman.

QM. An ottoman?

KERR. An ottoman.

QM. Well, I hope someone cleaned it up.

KERR. Of course, ma'am.

QM. Or perhaps in these straitened times you expect me to put on a pair of Marigolds –

KERR. No, ma'am.

QM. Do you expect me to take to my knees, Mr Kerr?

KERR. No, ma'am, of course not, ma'am.

QM. Because I can. I will if that is what you are asking. Take me to the ottoman, it will be my new crusade.

KERR. I wouldn't dream, ma'am. It is taken care of.

QM. Well, then I am not quite sure what this has to do with me?

KERR. No, ma'am… if I may: I fear this has something to do with Billy.

QM. Billy? Whatever do you mean? You're not suggesting he did something to the Harrington-Bahrs?

KERR. I have my suspicions.

QM. Do you now?

KERR. I'm afraid so, ma'am.

QM. Do you have any proof?

KERR. Ma'am, it was all very well when he was simply a footman, ma'am, but I worry he is taking advantage of his new position.

QM. Never. Besides I'm sure you will find ways to 'contain' him.

KERR. Ma'am, it is a serious business.

QM. Oh is it? Is it serious?

KERR. The palace is concerned.

QM. When are they not these days?

KERR. I fear he is a danger, ma'am. I can't make head or tail of his bookkeeping, he hires all and sundry without consultation, there is a recklessness, a heedlessness.

QM. He heeds me.

KERR. I fear he takes advantage of your kindness.

QM. My kindness is overstated. Billy understands his position. His role. Perhaps you are unaware as you have only just joined us, Mr Kerr.

KERR. I've been here seven years, ma'am.

QM. Exactly, it's all very new to you. Billy has been with us for twenty-five years. He walks the line, I grant you, but he knows not to go too far.

KERR. Does he? I'm not so sure and in the light of today's budgetary assessment I do wonder if we need to look at the level of staffing more generally.

QM. This is not a negotiation, Mr Kerr. I have had quite enough of that today.

Beat.

Is this what is to become of us, I wonder? My mother-in-law was obsessed by the threat of revolution, the mob on the street, but I fear we are to be picked apart instead; picked apart piece by piece by middle managers; men called Nigel and Kevin – and what is your first name?

KERR. Jeremy.

QM. Jeremy, thank you; carrion birds in cheap, grey suits encircling the remains of a once-great institution. Mark my words: every peck of their beak just emboldens another peck and another. We may look well look up one day and find ourselves reduced to mere skin and bones and wonder where it all started. Does it start here, Jeremy, does it start here?

KERR. Yes, ma'am. No, ma'am.

QM. After all if we are not a royal family, and treated as such, what are we?

KERR *doesn't know how to answer.*

That will be all.

He nods his head.

The QM *walks out of the room.*

KERR *is left on his own. He seethes and, after a moment, exits.*

Almost immediately, BILLY *and* GWYDION *enter from a different door and start clearing/cleaning.*

BILLY. You were not terrible today.

GWYDION. Thank you, sir.

BILLY. I think perhaps I'll keep you.

GWYDION. Very good, sir.

They continue to clear the set.

BILLY. What are your plans later?

GWYDION. Maybe a drink with the lads.

BILLY. The lads? How very *Boys' Own*. How thrilling.

GWYDION. To welcome me. They said there's a ritual of sorts.

BILLY. Oh yes, the 'ritual'. Well, I suppose you have to go to that.

Beat.

But perhaps you could stop by my room after.

GWYDION. It could be quite late, sir?

BILLY. That's not necessarily a problem. I'm something of a night owl.

GWYDION (*keeping it professional*). Did you need me for something, sir? Perhaps I can do it now instead.

BILLY. Oh no, never mind, I can manage on my own. I always have. Besides I may go for a walk.

GWYDION. At night, sir?

BILLY. Best time for it. The things you find. You should try it.

GWYDION. Do you not get lost?

BILLY. Lost? Never. I can see in the dark, you see.

Beat.

GWYDION. Can I ask a question, sir?

BILLY. The answer to that is usually 'no'.

GWYDION. You won't get in trouble, will you? For the drinks?

BILLY. Oh, no, Daff; you see there are two queens in this castle.

GWYDION laughs.

(*Serious*.) And I suggest you pay attention to them both, equally. Yes?

GWYDION hesitates.

KERR enters, furious.

Ah, Mr Kerr.

KERR (*pointing at* GWYDION). Out.

GWYDION exits.

The two men look at each other, not backing down.

BILLY. Is there something amiss, Mr Kerr?

KERR. I think so. I certainly think so. I fear a rot.

BILLY. A rat? Where?

KERR. A rot. I am talking of a rot that is taking hold in this place.

BILLY. There's terrible damp in the staff quarters but I assume you're not talking about that.

KERR. Enough!

BILLY. Whatever is the matter, Mr Kerr?

KERR. The Harrington-Bahrs have taken ill.

BILLY. Have they? (*Innocently.*) Do we know what caused it?

KERR. Yes.

Beat.

BILLY. I wonder if it is perhaps something they ate. Shall I speak to the kitchen? Was it the canapés do we think?

KERR. We do not.

BILLY. It is a mystery then.

KERR. I have spoken to her majesty.

BILLY. And what does her majesty say?

KERR. Well… she is appalled, naturally.

BILLY. Naturally…

KERR. And agrees with me that something must be done.

BILLY. Oh yes something must… but what?

KERR. Exactly… what? What do we do with you, Billy?

BILLY. Me?

KERR. I'm told you are considered amusing.

BILLY. How kind.

KERR. But I don't find you funny at all. At all. And this famous charm. What is it?

BILLY. What is charm? Well if you don't know I'm not sure I can teach you.

KERR. I'm not asking you to teach me.

BILLY. I could though. I could perhaps ease the way between you and her majesty.

KERR. You? How dare you? Her majesty and I are… We are… This is absurd.

BILLY. Perhaps flowers?

KERR. Flowers! What have flowers got to do with anything?

BILLY (*moving away from* KERR, *considering the vases of flowers*). So cheering to the sick. Perhaps a spray of pink roses for our patients? Not everyone can keep up with her majesty, you see. She runs rings around me, perhaps Mr and Mrs Crushing-Bore just simply couldn't keep up?

KERR. You enjoy words, don't you, Billy?

BILLY. Do I?

KERR. Yes, the sound of them mostly, like a prattling child when they first learn to speak. It's all a game, it's all a pun to you. But I'm going to tell you something, something I would have thought you would have learnt by now, something that doesn't normally even have to be said in this country: words don't matter. They don't matter a jot. We all pretend they do, of course, but anyone can learn words. Parrots can learn words, it doesn't mean they are capable of independent thought. And it doesn't even matter how well you speak them because anyone can change their accent – absolutely *anyone* – but that doesn't mean they *are* someone. Do you understand me? We always know, we can always tell…

BILLY. What can you tell?

KERR. Whether you are one of us.

BILLY. One of us?

KERR. There you go again. Parroting. What a pretty polly parrot. It doesn't matter how far you rise, Billy, you will never, ever belong.

BILLY *advances on* KERR *in a sudden motion.* KERR *flinches.* BILLY *stops and starts to walk towards an exit.*

Careful, Billy. You reveal yourself.

BILLY *continues towards the exit.*

FOOTMEN *and* MAIDS *enter in an elegant formation. They start to cover the furniture in dust sheets as the light darkens around them.*

Lights down.

Scene Three

Same location. Lights up. 1952.

The QM *enters the room from the opposite entrance in mourning dress. She stands looking at the ghostly furniture. She sighs, then lets herself weep.*

YOUNG BILLY *(fifteen) enters, unaware of her presence.*

Embarrassed by her tears, she goes upstage.

YOUNG BILLY *starts taking off the dust sheets, while humming.*

After a moment he catches sight of the QM.

He falls to the ground in a bow.

YOUNG BILLY. I'm sorry, your majesty, I didn't see you.

She turns.

QM. That's quite all right. I was hiding.

YOUNG BILLY. Is there anything I can get you, ma'am?

QM. No, I don't think so. I'm just… Well I don't know really. I seem to have become someone who enters a room for no reason and, for lack of anything to do, stays.

YOUNG BILLY. Would you like me to leave, ma'am?

QM. No, no, carry on. Carry on.

BILLY *nods his head and continues to reveal the furniture.*

It's terribly gloomy.

He goes to the window and opens the curtains.

Well, at least it's got four walls and a roof.

YOUNG BILLY *goes to the sofa and starts plumping the pillows.*

The QM *goes to the sofa and sits.*

He steps back.

Do I know you?

YOUNG BILLY. No, ma'am.

QM. Strangers everywhere. You're very young, aren't you? How old are you?

YOUNG BILLY. Fifteen, ma'am.

QM. Are we reduced to kidnapping? Shouldn't you be at school?

YOUNG BILLY. No, ma'am. I would have come sooner, ma'am.

QM. What do you mean?

YOUNG BILLY. I've been writing since I was twelve.

QM. To me?

YOUNG BILLY. Yes, ma'am. You and the late king.

QM. How queer. About what?

YOUNG BILLY. Working here.

QM. Working at the palace you mean? I expect you would prefer to still be in the palace.

YOUNG BILLY. No, ma'am.

QM. I don't believe you.

YOUNG BILLY. I have asked to come with you to Clarence House, now you're… here.

QM. And have I said yes?

YOUNG BILLY. Yes, ma'am.

QM. How clever of me… I imagine you are already regretting the decision.

YOUNG BILLY. No, ma'am.

QM. It will take a lot to make it into anything at all. And we're quite out of the way from everything. An ambitious young man like yourself? Are you sure you're not better off serving… her majesty?

YOUNG BILLY. No I don't think so… your majesty.

He nods his head.

QM. Let me look at you.

BILLY *stands up taller.*

You are small.

YOUNG BILLY. Yes, ma'am.

QM. Will you grow?

YOUNG BILLY. Only if your majesty wills it.

She laughs.

QM. You've made me laugh.

YOUNG BILLY. I'm sorry, ma'am.

QM. So you should be.

QM. What is your name?

YOUNG BILLY. Billy, ma'am.

QM. And where are you from, young man?

YOUNG BILLY *hesitates.*

You may speak freely. There is after all no rush. No rush about anything any more.

YOUNG BILLY. Coventry, ma'am.

QM. Yes, I can hear the accent now.

YOUNG BILLY. Apologies, ma'am. I am working on my vowels.

QM. Don't apologise. One can't help where one is born. Or one's station, of course. The trick to happiness is to be content where one is. Or so I am told.

YOUNG BILLY. Yes, ma'am. I'm sorry, ma'am.

QM. But I suspect you were not content in Coventry.

YOUNG BILLY. Not fully, ma'am. It's very…

QM. Go on.

YOUNG BILLY. Grey, ma'am. Small and grey.

QM. I see. What do your parents do?

YOUNG BILLY. They run a shop, ma'am.

QM. What sort?

YOUNG BILLY. Hardware, ma'am. Hammers and nails and whatnot.

QM. Well yes, I suppose people have need of hardware, hence a shop, yes it all makes perfect sense when you think about it. But you did not fancy a life amongst hammers and nails and whatnot?

YOUNG BILLY. No, ma'am. It wasn't for me.

QM. Are you the creative sort then?

YOUNG BILLY. Ma'am?

QM. Because there is nothing terribly creative in service, be warned.

YOUNG BILLY. Yes, ma'am, but I like that there is a proper way of doing things.

QM. Quite right. So few young people do though these days.

YOUNG BILLY. I wouldn't want to be anywhere else, ma'am.

QM. Have you really been writing to me for years?

YOUNG BILLY. Yes, ma'am.

QM. Whatever for?

YOUNG BILLY. You are the queen.

QM (*matter of fact*). The Queen is the queen now, since the king died, I am simply Queen Elizabeth, the Queen's mother – it's come a little sooner than anyone expected but there it is. There it is.

Pause.

No but you see not every twelve-year-old in the country writes to me year after year. The more I think about it the more I find it rather extraordinary. Why us? Why me?

YOUNG BILLY. Because you are extraordinary, ma'am.

QM (*defensive*). Oh stop that. I won't have that.

YOUNG BILLY. I mean it, ma'am. You have always been extraordinary to me. Ever since I was little I used to imagine…

QM. No go on. You've started now.

YOUNG BILLY. I used to imagine this conversation.

QM. The one we're having now?

YOUNG BILLY. No, ma'am. A bit better.

QM. My apologies, am I not keeping up?

YOUNG BILLY. No I mean… in my daydream I would know exactly what to say and I would say it better than I am right now.

QM (*softening*). You're doing very well. What else happened in this dream?

YOUNG BILLY. I would do something or say something and it would please you.

QM. And then what?

YOUNG BILLY. That's it, ma'am.

QM. Well. Well… you have. Well done.

YOUNG BILLY. Thank you, ma'am.

QM. How does that make you feel, Billy?

YOUNG BILLY. It is the proudest moment of my life, ma'am.

QM. You have the shining eyes of a religious zealot. Do you know what that means?

YOUNG BILLY. No, ma'am.

QM. No neither do I yet.

Beat.

Now. Do you know how to mix a drink?

YOUNG BILLY. Of course, ma'am.

QM. I'll be the judge of that.

The lights darken, flicker.

They exit.

Scene Four

As in Scene One. April. 1979. The Garden Room. Later that night.

On a side table, a handful of charming decorated cardboard boxes and some objects. It should feel like someone has been wrapping presents.

BILLY *enters, he looks offstage where you sense someone is waiting.*

BILLY. Please do come in. We don't bite. Or at the least very rarely.

IAN *enters (late twenties/thirty, Black). He wears jeans and a tight T-shirt and boots.*

IAN. Are you sure it's okay for us to be in here?

IAN *looks about the room.*

Fuck me.

BILLY. Well, quite.

BILLY *pulls* IAN *towards him and starts kissing him.*

It gets more passionate and IAN *steps back, disturbing a piece of furniture.*

BILLY *pulls away.*

IAN. Sorry.

BILLY *nods.*

An uncertainty has been introduced.

IAN *wanders around the room.*

BILLY. What do you think of it?

IAN. It'll do.

BILLY. Yes, that is also her majesty's view. Of course, she was used to living in an actual palace before here.

IAN. Where?

BILLY. Buckingham Palace. When she was queen.

IAN. Before my time.

BILLY. Well, yes.

IAN. And you can just come and go?

BILLY. Indeed.

IAN. You've got the keys?

BILLY. Figuratively and literally.

IAN. You're the butler.

BILLY. Even better, darling, I'm Page of the Backstairs.

IAN. I bet you are. Billy Big Bollocks.

BILLY. Billy Big Bollocks, that's rather good.

IAN. How long have you been doing that?

BILLY. Two weeks but I have been in service for the family for nearly thirty years.

IAN. Took you long enough.

BILLY. I am the youngest page in living memory. My ascendency is astonishing.

SCENE FOUR 53

IAN. Is it now?

BILLY. Tart.

IAN. What are these?

He goes to the side table with the boxes and objects.

BILLY. These are icebreakers for our guests tomorrow. Guests are so awfully nervous when they come for an event and speak all sorts of impersonal nonsense to her majesty and if there is one thing she can't abide it's small talk. So these are objects which may stimulate discussion. For example, we have a childhood friend of her majesty coming, Lady Adeline, they came out together. So here is the pressed flower her majesty wore on her presentation to her majesty Queen Mary in 1922. Isn't that nice?

IAN, *ignoring the question, touches a curtain.*

Damask. Silk.

IAN. Bit pink.

BILLY. Oh really?

IAN. The décor, it's a bit –

BILLY. Décor? Well la-di-da. She speaks French.

IAN. It is a bit naff.

BILLY. Because your bedsit, I assume, in Balham?

IAN. Tooting.

BILLY. Dear God, even worse – is the height of chic? A mattress on the floor and sheets for curtains hardly counts as minimalism, darling.

IAN. No, it's nice.

BILLY. Nice? Nice? This is Clarence bloody House! Home of the Queen Mother, the most popular person in Britain, former Queen Consort and the last Empress of India.

IAN. Yes, as I said: nice. Just a little… 'gauche'.

BILLY. Gauche?

IAN. Gauche.

BILLY. Darling, as a rule I don't take interior-design advice from boys I pick up head down, arse up from a urinal trough in Piccadilly.

IAN. You're missing out.

BILLY. Clearly.

IAN. Does she sit here?

BILLY. She has been known to sit there, yes.

IAN. Doing what?

BILLY. Reading. Occasionally entertaining but working really, she never really stops working.

IAN laughs.

What?

IAN. Nothing, carry on.

BILLY. She works tremendously hard.

IAN. If you say so.

BILLY. She isn't at all how you think.

IAN. To be honest, I don't really think about her at all.

Beat.

BILLY. You can sit if you want.

IAN. Really?

BILLY. Of course.

BILLY considers it.

IAN. You bring a lot of boys back here?

BILLY. No.

IAN. Yeah, you do.

BILLY. Not in here normally.

IAN. I'm special am I?

BILLY. Not exactly.

IAN. A special occasion?

BILLY. A long day.

> IAN *looks at him again*.
>
> It clearly doesn't impress you though.

IAN. It's not like you actually own it. All this. You just work here.

BILLY. And what do you do exactly?

IAN. I work for myself.

BILLY. Tricking doesn't count as a small business last time I checked.

IAN. Well, it's not small, darling.

BILLY. Charming.

IAN. And I only do that now and then.

BILLY. What else you do you do?

IAN. I'm an artist.

BILLY. How wonderful.

IAN. I am.

BILLY. I'm sure you are.

IAN. I've studied.

BILLY. Have you exhibited anywhere?

IAN. Not anywhere you would go, no.

BILLY. Darling, are you annoyed?

IAN. Why do you say that?

BILLY. Because you seem a little angry.

IAN. I expect we all seem angry to you.

BILLY. Oh no, no, I don't do that.

IAN. What?

BILLY. Politics.

IAN. Clearly.

BILLY. When I look at you all I see is beauty. A savage beauty.

IAN *stands up.*

IAN. Would you like to see one of my pieces?

BILLY. Your 'pieces'? Absolutely.

IAN *goes to his backpack. With ceremony, he pulls out a giant black porcelain rod with zigzag dayglo markings up the side. Maybe punk safety pins piercing. It looks like a totem pole. It looks like a giant dildo.*

Gosh.

IAN. I'm interested in the objectification and fetishisation of the Black male member in Western art and contemporary culture.

BILLY. Do you know what? So am I.

IAN. Yes, I thought you might be.

IAN *hands him the sculpture.*

I call it Black Dawn... II.

BILLY. Oh it's a sequel.

IAN. It is.

BILLY. I must have missed the first one. Did you actually make this?

IAN. Of course I did.

BILLY. It's actually rather well made.

IAN. Is it 'actually'?

BILLY. No I rather like it.

IAN. Do you?

BILLY. I do, I do.

Beat.

How many inches is it exactly?

IAN. It's not a cock. It's a lightning rod. (*Off* BILLY*'s look.*) Or it's a cock and a lightning rod. It has the power to channel lightning and crack the earth wide open.

BILLY. Right.

IAN. Does it make you uncomfortable?

BILLY. Well, it would if I sat on it but not really. Should it?

IAN snatches it from him and puts it on the side table with the other 'objets'.

And have you sold many?

IAN. I have had interest.

BILLY. How much does interest pay?

IAN. Not a lot but it's not about the money.

BILLY. So, you're what, on the dole?

IAN. And? It's my right.

BILLY. Well, I wouldn't know about that. I've always worked. I've been working here since I was fifteen.

IAN. Here?

BILLY. Here.

IAN. Fuck me. But that explains a lot.

BILLY. Does it?

IAN. It's like you've been frozen in time. You and that old lady.

BILLY. That old lady? The problem is your generation can only think of her as an old woman. Your nan, only posher. Soft. Softness incarnate. A gentle smile. A slow wave. All in a gentle pastel wash. Yes, yes. The Queen Mum. (*With disdain.*) Mum. She is not *your* mum; she is the Queen's mother and before that the Queen of England. She refused to leave London even as the bombs battered the streets you now swish along. She risked her life for this country and then when peace came, she had but a few brief years and then it was all snatched away in a moment; her husband, her title, her home. All gone. Even her daughter, in a sense. Never to remarry, always to stand and wave and smile even when she must have been in the most terrible pain. She is a national symbol of resilience and serenity.

IAN. You believe that, don't you?

BILLY. I do. I would have started even younger if I could've. When I was finally taken on I felt freed.

IAN. Freed to serve?

BILLY. Darling, if you had any idea what it was like in the fifties we wouldn't be having this conversation. The palace was practically the only, the only place, the only place with the faintest trace of glamour and the only place people like us could be together.

IAN. People like us.

BILLY (*lowers his voice*). Queers.

IAN. Darling, we are not the same.

Beat.

Things are changing you know.

BILLY (*bitter*). Oh I know.

IAN. For the better. You don't have to hide behind a queen to be a queen any more.

BILLY. Is that what you think I'm doing?

IAN. Aren't you?

BILLY. I am William Tallon, Page of the Backstairs, Chief Steward to Queen Elizabeth, lords and ladies, princes, prime ministers all know my name.

IAN. So?

BILLY. So? What are you?

IAN. I told you: I'm an artist. I don't need to be anything else. I don't need anyone else.

BILLY *stops himself and moves to the other side of the space.*

Silence.

Gone quiet, have you? Scared she's going to walk in?

BILLY. Hardly. Are you?

IAN. Not me. It's you that would be in trouble, not me.

BILLY. I would. Lots of trouble.

IAN (*picking up on the vibe*). Bringing me in here, a stranger, sneaking me in past the guards.

BILLY. They know me, of course.

IAN. Barely looked up.

BILLY. They know I'm not to be questioned.

IAN. Billy Big Bollocks, aren't you?

BILLY. You could say that, that's actually rather good.

IAN. Shut up.

BILLY. Yes, sir.

IAN. You'd be in a lot of trouble I'd say if they found us.

BILLY. I would. I would if she found me on my knees.

IAN. On your knees, exactly.

BILLY *goes down on his knees.*

Shit, you are naughty, aren't you?

BILLY. You have no idea.

He reaches for IAN*'s flies.*

IAN. Here?

BILLY. Why not?

IAN. Is she… in?

BILLY. No, she's popped out for a packet of fags.

He starts to undo IAN's *flies*.

IAN. Wait.

Beat.

You don't have to impress me, mate. We can go to your room.

BILLY. I'm not trying to impress you.

IAN. If you got caught though.

BILLY. Her majesty is fast asleep.

IAN. She's not the only one who lives here though, is she?

BILLY. She's the only one that matters. Everyone else I can manage.

IAN. Think you're Billy Big Bollocks, don't you?

BILLY. I am Billy Big Bollocks.

IAN *looks around then, after a moment, undoes his flies.*

Footsteps.

The door being pushes and pulled.

They freeze, then panic. The door opens.

In the doorway is framed what looks like a shadow with a tiara.

A moment of suspense before the shadow with a tiara reveals itself to be GWYDION *in only his Y-front pants (or less) and a party crown. He runs into the space, clearly drunk, clearly being chased.*

IAN *and* BILLY *spring apart.*

Gwydion?

SCENE FOUR

GWYDION *stops, caught and confused.*

GWYDION. Sir. I'm sorry, sir.

He tries to cover himself.

IAN. What's going on?

BILLY. The ritual. Every new footman has to make it across the house without being caught. Gwydion nearly made it.

IAN. And what happens if they're caught?

BILLY. They're fired.

IAN. You're not going to fire him, are you?

BILLY. Well, I should really. It is the rule.

GWYDION. Sir, please.

IAN. Gwydion is it? I'm Ian.

GWYDION. Nice to meet you, sir.

IAN. Don't call me sir. (*Teasing.*) Call me mate, or comrade, if you like.

BILLY. Ian is my… cousin.

IAN. Do that to all your cousins, do you?

BILLY (*all airs and graces*). And this is the Garden Room, Ian. But I do think perhaps it's time for us to wrap this up.

IAN (*queening it up*). Not what you said earlier.

BILLY *moves* IAN *away and then turns to* GWYDION.

BILLY. Daff?

GWYDION. Yes, sir.

BILLY. I didn't see anything.

GWYDION. Thank you, sir.

BILLY. And neither did you.

GWYDION. Yes, sir.

BILLY. Now cover yourself up and go back downstairs.

GWYDION. Thank you.

BILLY exits with IAN, who sneaks a look behind at GWYDION's ass. BILLY pulls him away.

GWYDION, now left to his own devices, looks around for something to cover himself.

He stands behind the sofa, which hides him and considers the soft furnishings. He picks up a cushion.

He then reconsiders – too small.

He decides on a small throw and just as he picks it up – another FOOTMAN bursts in, which causes GWYDION to spin around and knock over all the boxes and objects onto the floor.

FOOTMAN. Hurry up. I think I saw Billy.

GWYDION. Give us a hand.

They quickly pile the objects back into the boxes, including the dildo sculpture.

They exit the room, turning the light off as they go.

Interval.

Scene Five

Same location. The morning after the night before. BILLY *is organising breakfast things on a small table for the Queen Mother.*

She enters, he bows.

QM. Looking rather peaky, Billy. Are you ill?

BILLY. No, ma'am.

QM. Late one, was it?

BILLY. I couldn't possibly confirm or deny.

QM. Getting a bit old for that, aren't we?

BILLY. Undoubtedly, ma'am.

QM. Well, perk up. It's going to be a busy day and I need you on your toes. Margaret is popping by for breakfast.

BILLY. Oh really?

QM. Yes, I was surprised too. Her idea though, which I'm taking as a good sign. Although what I actually did to end up in the doghouse I'm not entirely sure. But perhaps this is an *entente cordiale*?

BILLY. Is that with or without vermouth?

QM. Oh very good. Then I hear a ribbon needs cutting somewhere in…?

BILLY. Surrey.

QM. Could be worse. Could be…?

BILLY. The North?

QM. Exactly. A leisure centre in Surrey. A centre for leisure. Can you imagine such a thing?

BILLY. No, ma'am.

QM. Have people stopped work entirely?

BILLY. Yes, ma'am.

QM. Eggs?

BILLY. Yes, ma'am.

QM. Overdone?

BILLY. I had words with the kitchen.

QM. Terrible words?

BILLY. Unspeakable. Threats of the Tower, disembowelment.

He lifts up the serving dish to reveal some hard-boiled eggs.

QM. We shall see.

She sits down.

Yes, I think it's rather nice Margaret is joining us again for breakfasts.

BILLY. Very nice.

QM. I do hope she's not late though. I'm getting hungry – (*Referring to the eggs.*) and I have a bad feeling about these… (*She gestures to her eggs.*)

BILLY. The papers, ma'am, while you wait?

QM. Certainly not.

BILLY. Yes, ma'am.

She waits.

QM. You're quiet.

BILLY. Am I, ma'am? My apologies.

QM. Don't apologise, just cheer up. I am determined to have a good day. Everything and everyone is far too dour and doomy these days, have you noticed?

BILLY. Yes, ma'am.

The door to reveal the FOOTMAN *we saw earlier.*

QM. Ah-ha. There she is.

The FOOTMAN *hands* BILLY *a note.* BILLY *reads it.*

BILLY *looks grave.*

BILLY. I'm afraid Princess Margaret has been delayed, ma'am.

QM. For how long?

BILLY. I think it's a matter of rescheduling the breakfast.

QM. To when?

BILLY. She does not say.

QM. Cancelling, you mean? Oh that is… That is quite the thing, isn't it? It was her idea! I didn't ask her to visit.

BILLY. I'm sure she sends her apologies.

QM. Are you? Does she? I was perfectly content on my own. Perfectly content.

She sighs.

Silence as the QM *mouths a conversation to herself but doesn't speak aloud.*

After a moment.

Yes, well, there it is. Everyone's very busy I'm sure.

She cracks open her egg. It's overdone.

She yelps/screams.

Does she throw it?

BILLY. I'm so sorry, ma'am.

QM (*raising her voice*). What is the point?

BILLY. I know, I know.

QM. What is the point?

He takes away the egg.

QM. What is the point of being a bloody queen if my own children stand me up and I can't even get a half-decent egg. I could go to a greasy spoon in… in in?

BILLY. Kennington?

QM. Exactly. And maybe I should.

BILLY. It can be arranged.

QM. Maybe it should. Maybe it should.

BILLY. I know just the place on Brixton Road. Fry-up. Pie and mash and gravy.

QM. Wonderful. Let's go! Right now.

BILLY. Yes, ma'am.

QM. Go and tell Kerr – the day is cancelled.

BILLY. Yes, ma'am.

QM. Don't take no for an answer. Leisure centre be damned.

BILLY. Certainly, ma'am.

They smile at each other but neither moves. They've been here before.

QM. Take this all away. I'm finished with it.

He starts moving the plates to a sideboard.

It's just as well Margaret was ill, the eggs would have pushed her over the edge. We would have had our first beheading in three hundred and fifty-five years.

BILLY (*Margaret impression*). 'Well if those eggs are not a heinous act of treason I don't know what is.'

QM. Is that supposed to be Margaret?

BILLY. Apologies, ma'am.

QM. No it's rather good. Do you do any others?

BILLY. No, ma'am.

QM. I think you do.

BILLY. I have gone too far. Overstepped.

QM. Charles?

BILLY (*Charles impression*). 'Well, if I am forced to say a few words then I suppose I must. And by a few I mean a thousand.'

She laughs.

QM. Oh now that is good. It's like he's here.

BILLY. 'And how are you this morning, Grandma?'

QM. Gan-Gan.

BILLY. Gan-Gan.

QM. Deserted. Abandoned. You don't come to see me any more. None of you do.

BILLY. Well, I've been rather busy.

QM. Yes, I've seen… in the papers.

BILLY. Don't believe any of that.

QM. I don't. Of course I don't. It's rubbish, anyone can see that. I do rather wish there was a bit less of it though.

BILLY. Yes, Gan-Gan. But the papers do make a fuss if I'm even seen in public with a woman.

QM. Time to find a nice girl. A simple girl, a young girl, I think would be best for you now, Charles.

BILLY. Yes, I think so.

QM. You do? Excellent, I will think on who. But I'll need lots of great-grandchildren before I get old and senile. (*Breaking character.*) I miss children around, don't you, Billy?

BILLY. Not particularly, ma'am.

QM. I do, terribly. They are good boys though, aren't they? Men now, of course. I shall feel better when they're married and settled though. Then I'll be able to relax.

BILLY. Yes, ma'am.

He has picked up the breakfast tray and is moving towards the door.

QM. I better get ready for the leisure centre. I hope they don't expect me to get in the pool.

BILLY. Would you like me to pack a towel?

QM. Well, yes I'd think you better had.

BILLY. Tomorrow I shall watch them cook the egg and time it myself.

QM. Yes I think you better.

BILLY. Is that all?

QM. Yes, that's all.

He goes towards the door.

Billy?

BILLY. Yes, ma'am.

QM. Thank you. You are a boon to me, Billy, you know that.

The QM *exits.*

BILLY. I do and it is my pleasure.

KERR *enters,* BILLY *sees and goes to exit.*

KERR. Ah Billy, when you have a minute.

BILLY. Can't stop now, Mr Kerr. Terribly busy. Trying to locate her majesty's beach towel.

KERR. Her what?

BILLY. It really is most urgent.

BILLY *exits, as* GWYDION *enters and starts clearing plates.*

KERR. Gwydion, is it?

GWYDION. Yes, sir.

KERR. You remind me of a chap I knew in the war.

GWYDION. Is that right, sir?

KERR. Nice boy; well brought up, polite, hopeful. Died, of course. You have a similar doomed quality, which is really very appealing. Has anyone ever told you that?

GWYDION. Yes, actually, I get told that a lot here.

KERR. And how are you getting on?

GWYDION. Good, thank you.

KERR. Good. Very good. So, you like it here?

GWYDION. I do.

KERR. I have heard promising things. Not everyone is cut out for service. You can't be too stupid or clever actually but you're presentable and affable and have the face of a fallen soldier; you could go far. If you want to. Do you want to?

GWYDION. I do like it here, sir.

KERR. Good. Just keep your head about you and steer clear of certain elements.

GWYDION. Elements?

KERR. Yes, I'm afraid everything you hear about London is true. A den of vice, a city of drinkers, gamblers, and homosexuals.

GWYDION. Homosexuals, sir?

KERR. Avoid them like the plague.

GWYDION *keeps quiet*.

Seems like every year there is more and more and not just in the usual places. Very bold they're getting, protesting even. I mean, what more do they want? To marry? They are even, of course, working here.

GWYDION. Are they, sir?

KERR. Is that something you've noticed?

GWYDION. I wouldn't know what they looked like, sir.

KERR. Is that right? Very good. And how do you find Billy?

GWYDION. In what way, sir?

KERR. Whatever way you like?

GWYDION. He's funny.

KERR. He's a clown.

GWYDION. Her majesty is very keen on him.

KERR. That is unfortunate. He's not your friend, Gwydion. He's a cuckoo bird.

GWYDION *keeps quiet*.

I'm going to be direct, Gwydion, as we are both straight-talking men of the world: is Billy abusing his privileges and the trust the Queen Mother has given him? Because that, in the end, is the most important thing: trust.

BILLY *appears, notices the intimacy*.

BILLY. Kerr. Still here?

KERR. You can't get rid of me.

BILLY. So it appears.

KERR. I'll speak with you later.

BILLY. Yes, sir.

KERR *exits*.

What did she want?

GWYDION. Nothing, sir.

BILLY. Good. Where are the boxes?

GWYDION. I took them into the Lancaster Room.

BILLY. Make sure they're properly labelled for later.

GWYDION. Yes, sir.

Beat.

Sir?

BILLY. Yes, Dafne.

GWYDION. About last night.

BILLY. What about it?

GWYDION. I've been thinking about your friend.

BILLY. My cousin?

GWYDION. Not sure that makes it better.

BILLY. Makes what better?

GWYDION. What I saw.

BILLY. And what did you see?

GWYDION. Not much.

BILLY. Correct.

GWYDION. Potentially.

BILLY. Do you know what I saw last night? Not much either.

Beat.

Is that what Kerr was asking about?

GWYDION. I didn't say anything.

BILLY. Good boy.

GWYDION. But I have been thinking.

BILLY. Dangerous.

GWYDION. Me and a few other footmen have been talking.

BILLY. Thinking *and* talking. Worrying. About what? What do you want?

GWYDION. Pay and conditions.

Beat.

BILLY. So, it's true then? You really are Welsh.

GWYDION. Diolch yn fawr – (*Ironically.*) 'boyo'.

He exits, leaving BILLY *on his own.*

Blackout.

Scene Six

Later that afternoon. Garden Room, Clarence House. The QM *walks through the space with* BILLY *and* KERR.

QM. And what is on the itinerary this afternoon?

BILLY. Drinks, ma'am.

QM. Oh very good.

KERR. And how was the opening of the leisure centre, ma'am?

QM. Well, let's just say they weren't expecting the bikini.

They don't know how to respond.

That was a joke.

The men laugh.

I am clearly losing my touch. It was fine, it was in…?

BILLY. Brentford.

QM. Which is a place apparently.

KERR. And then there's the reception this afternoon.

QM. Which we are looking forward to. No old farts at all, I believe.

KERR. I wouldn't know, ma'am.

QM. There's Adeline though of course, she must be getting up there.

KERR. I understand she is rather…

QM. Dotty?

KERR. Ma'am.

QM. Yes, so they tell me but I can't really tell the difference. She always was rather touched. But glass houses and all that.

KERR *shuffles uncomfortably.*

Oh don't be squeamish, Kerr. Who else is coming?

BILLY. Largely known quantities. Lady Miffie Astlebury.

QM. Well, I shan't have to say a word then.

BILLY. And Hugo McCoyd.

QM. Dear Hugo. He will pretend to still be in love with me and I will pretend to believe him. How wonderful we managed to put together a function without an emissary from Snorezania or some such.

They laugh too hard.

Don't patronise me, boys.

She goes to exit.

KERR. I do believe there is a late addition to the party. An emissary from the royal delegation from Lesotho.

QM. Oh well, that could be jolly.

KERR. Yes, ma'am.

QM. Do you have that covered, Billy?

KERR. Yes, Billy, do you have that covered, Billy?

BILLY. When have I not had it covered?

KERR. I've heard about the eggs.

BILLY. That is the fault of the kitchen.

KERR. Of which you are in charge.

QM. Will you two queens stop bickering? This queen wants a drink.

Enter a young FOOTMAN *with a letter.*

FOOTMAN (*to* BILLY). Sir?

BILLY. What?

FOOTMAN. A note, sir.

The QM *and* KERR *exit into the corridor.*

A message from the palace. The royal delegation from Lesotho? He's been delayed.

BILLY. Fine.

FOOTMAN. And there's someone here who says he wants to speak. Says he knows you.

BILLY. Everyone knows me.

FOOTMAN. Says he's your cousin.

BILLY. Ah.

FOOTMAN. But he's...

He gestures to his face.

BILLY. Send him in. Quickly.

He leaves.

BILLY *panics, then recovers, pulling it back in.*

A knock on the door.

Come in.

We see the FOOTMAN *and* IAN *behind.*

IAN *enters. The* FOOTMAN *hovers.*

Off. (*To* IAN.) Him, not you.

The door closes behind the FOOTMAN.

What do you want?

IAN. Not very friendly.

BILLY. How did you get in here?

IAN. I said I was your cousin, they said you had a lot of cousins, I said yes, and they let me in. Someone really must do something about your security. I could be anyone. I could have a knife.

BILLY. Do you have a knife?

IAN. Bog off.

BILLY. I'm rather busy.

IAN. I want Black Dawn.

BILLY. Then you have come to wrong place.

IAN. I left it here.

BILLY. Oh, you mean…

IAN. My sculpture. I've had some interest.

BILLY. I bet you have.

IAN. From a gallery.

BILLY. Really?

IAN. Yes, really. I wasn't lying. I'm an artist.

BILLY. And that's it? That's all you want.

IAN. That and twenty thousand pounds or I go to the press.

BILLY looks alarmed.

I just want my work back. But now you mention it –

BILLY. Stay here. Talk to nobody.

BILLY exits out of one of the side doors.

Almost immediately, KERR enters, walks through the space. Notices IAN. Double-takes, carries on walking and then stops, comes back.

KERR. Excuse me.

IAN. Why?

KERR. Are you…?

IAN.…

BILLY re-enters.

BILLY. Well, I can't find your dild–

He sees KERR.

Oh.

Beat.

(*To* KERR.) Hello.

KERR. Is this?

BILLY. Yes?

KERR. Who is this?

BILLY. This is…

IAN. Ian.

BILLY. Ian.

KERR raises his eyebrow.

KERR. And who is Ian?

A FOOTMAN enters.

FOOTMAN. The guests are ready, sir.

BILLY *(improvising)*. Ian is a guest.

Beat.

KERR. Were we expecting you?

BILLY. Yes, Ian is the late addition from the palace.

KERR. Oh of course, the royal delegation from Lesotho.

BILLY. Exactly. Yes, Ian is… a… prince.

KERR. Of course. My apologies, your highness.

IAN *(putting on a fairly spot-on Prince Charles impression with some deliberately clichéd African inflections)*. Not at all, old chap. I'm not one for titles but it's quite true you know, where I'm from I'm the son of a king but in England I prefer to be known as a handy full-back, decent bowler, and a jolly good chap.

KERR. I really do apologise, your highness.

IAN. Not at all.

KERR. You play rugger?

IAN. I do.

KERR. Full-back you say? I'd have had you more down as a hooker.

BILLY (*under his breath*). Same.

KERR (*to* BILLY). What's that?

IAN (*covering*). I played at university.

KERR. Which one?

IAN. The other one.

KERR. Ha. When were you up?

IAN. Seventy to seventy-three.

KERR. Perhaps you know my godson?

IAN. Possibly but I'm afraid all white people look the same to me.

KERR. Right, yes, of course.

He acquiesces but doesn't move.

But I think perhaps I will stay today.

BILLY *does not look pleased*.

And help…

BILLY. Are you sure?

KERR. Quite sure.

BILLY. Very well.

BILLY *ushers* IAN *to the other side of the room*.

If you'll come with me, your highness.

IAN. Call me Ian, please.

BILLY (*sotto voce*). What are you doing?

IAN. Having fun, darling.

BILLY. Where did you learn to do that?

IAN. What if I said Cambridge seventy to seventy-three?

GWYDION *enters carrying a tray with the icebreakers.*

BILLY. Just try and keep out of the way and, when I signal, leave.

IAN. We'll see. I quite fancy a word with the Queen Mum.

BILLY. You what?

> GWYDION *sees* IAN, *gives out a little yelp of alarm and drops the tray.*

What's wrong?

GWYDION. Nothing, sir.

> BILLY *kneels down to help* GWYDION.

(*Whispered.*) What's happening?

BILLY. The crown prince of Lesotho is just a little early.

GWYDION. But –

BILLY (*whispered*). When I give the signal, get him out.

GWYDION. Me? How?

> *They move the tray over to a sideboard.*

BILLY. And hold the drinks until he's gone. Kerr is watching.

(*Breaking away.*) Mr Kerr, I think it's time.

> *The central door opens and the* FOOTMAN *leads some guests through:* MIFFIE ASTLEBURY (*twenties, socialite*); HUGO McCOYD (*seventies, old friend of the* QM).

Come in, yes, come in I don't bite. Much. Lady Astlebury, I presume.

MIFFIE. Lady Astlebury's my father, call me Miffie.

BILLY. How droll.

MIFFIE. And you're the famous Billy.

BILLY. Well, I wouldn't say famous.

MIFFIE. Backstairs Billy. I can't believe we haven't met yet. Is it true there are secret tunnels between and only you have the keys? The things you must have seen.

BILLY. And have you met Mr Kerr, the Queen Mother's private secretary?

MIFFIE. No, do I have to?

KERR. Charmed.

MIFFIE. Likewise.

BILLY. And Mr McCoyd, are you well?

HUGO (*cheerful*). Me? Oh, alive it seems.

BILLY. That is good news.

HUGO. Isn't it just? You wouldn't believe how many people aren't these days. And is her majesty…?

BILLY. Very well.

HUGO. I heard a rumour about a little…?

BILLY. Untrue.

HUGO. Thank God. I cannot bear to think of a world without her.

BILLY. It would be unimaginable.

HUGO. Of course, for me there is a special significance.

MIFFIE. Why?

HUGO. Oh it was all so long ago.

MIFFIE. How thrilling. Were you two lovers?

HUGO. Good heavens, I couldn't possibly talk about that.

BILLY. I wonder if you'd like some tea, Mr McCoyd?

HUGO. Tea? I think a whisky would be preferable.

BILLY. It's rather early.

HUGO. Is it?

BILLY. And where is Lady Adeline?

FOOTMAN. She was just here.

He goes back into the corridor, followed by BILLY.

Sir?

BILLY *goes into the corridor.*

MIFFIE. Good Lord, who are you?

KERR. This is his royal highness, Prince Ian of –

IAN. Oh, please, just call me… sir! Ha.

MIFFIE (*sexual*). Yes, please.

BILLY (*off*). Lady Adeline, it's this way.

ADELINE (*off*). Don't be absurd I know exactly where I'm going.

BILLY *ushers in an older lady, with half an eye out for the real Lesotho delegation.*

BILLY. Here we are.

ADELINE. Where? But this is the Garden Room.

BILLY. Yes, that's right.

ADELINE. Of Clarence House?

BILLY. That's right.

ADELINE. But I'm here to meet the Queen.

MIFFIE. The Queen Mother, dearie.

ADELINE. What on earth is a Queen Mother? I'm here to see Elizabeth.

MIFFIE. Which one?

ADELINE. Well, not the Tudor one, obviously. Is she all right in the head, this one?

MIFFIE. Who, me? Not particularly.

ADELINE. Don't worry, dear, I'll look after you. My sister was also soft in the head you see.

HUGO (*to* IAN). Lady Adeline is… an old, old friend of –

ADELINE. Is that you, Hugo?

HUGO. Yes, Adeline, dear.

ADELINE. You look terrible.

HUGO. Terrible, that's quite true.

ADELINE. Old and fat.

HUGO. Terribly old and terribly fat.

ADELINE. You should do something about that. I weigh the same as I did on my wedding day.

MIFFIE. What is your secret?

ADELINE. Cigarettes.

MIFFIE. Mine too.

ADELINE. And if you're going to drink avoid food at all cost.

MIFFIE. Honestly, the wisdom of the ages right here.

HUGO. Talking of drink. Not that I need one of course, it's just if I don't have one soon the tremors kick in.

MIFFIE. Now tell me all about you, my young prince.

IAN. What would like to know?

MIFFIE. Where did you say you're from?

IAN. Lesotho.

MIFFIE. Don't know that one. Sorry.

IAN. Not at all! These African countries are always changing their names, it's so hard to keep up.

KERR (*warm agreement*). Isn't it? We were just saying that the other day.

IAN. Yes, well, fingers crossed it sticks. My father is doing his best.

KERR. Who is your –

IAN. The king. And president. So much more convenient that way.

KERR. Quite.

MIFFIE. Do they also worship you as a god? Because I would.

BILLY *wheels the trolley around at a rate of knots.*

KERR. Careful, Billy.

HUGO. What's this?

BILLY. Tea.

HUGO. Not this again.

BILLY. It's something we're experimenting with. Tea at teatime.

HUGO. Is it because of her majesty's health?

BILLY. Absolutely not.

HUGO. Because I have heard some things.

MIFFIE. What things have you heard exactly?

HUGO. I couldn't possibly say.

MIFFIE. Bowel, wasn't it?

KERR *and* BILLY *exchange panicked looks.*

BILLY. Tea, Lady Astlebury?

MIFFIE. Do I have to?

She takes a cup.

Budgetary, is it? Are we worried Labour will finally cut the cord?

HUGO. I'm rather hopeful about the Tories this year. This Thatcher has something about her.

MIFFIE. The grocer's daughter?

HUGO. That's right.

MIFFIE. God I hope not. She gives me the shivers. Besides, do we really want a woman in charge?

HUGO. Rather.

MIFFIE. I bet you would. He's filthy this one, are you filthy? I think you're filthy.

SCENE SIX

HUGO. I suspect the world would be a better place if the fairer sex took charge.

MIFFIE. So dull though, being in charge. Does the Queen have any fun, Billy? I rather feel like as the years have gone on she looks sadder and sadder while her mummy, who doesn't have to do anything, looks happier and happier.

HUGO. Radiant. Although she always had an inner glow.

MIFFIE. I dread to think what that Thatcher creature will look like in thirty years.

BILLY. Tea, Hugo?

HUGO. Well, if I must.

MIFFIE (*to* ADELINE). Did you two come out together, Lady Adeline?

ADELINE. I've only just got in.

MIFFIE. Honestly, though, what is your story, young man?

HUGO. Good point, do princes not dress up where you're from?

BILLY. Tea, Lady Adeline?

ADELINE. What time is it?

BILLY. Four p.m.

ADELINE. Shouldn't we be on the sherry by now?

HUGO. Hear, hear.

MIFFIE. Yes, come on, Billy, don't hold out on us. Frankly I only came for the booze. It's legendary.

BILLY. We are flattered.

MIFFIE. And what do you do when you're not being a prince?

IAN. I'm an artist.

MIFFIE. What luck. I work for a gallery in Mayfair. My clientele would go mad for an African prince, it would be too much, wouldn't it, Billy?

BILLY. Much too much.

MIFFIE What sort of thing do you do?

IAN. Sculpture.

MIFFIE. Oh lovely. Sculpture is so tremendously pointless and expensive.

IAN. I don't really do it for the money.

MIFFIE Of course you don't – even better. What's your subject?

BILLY. Cake, anyone?

IAN. The fetishisation and deification of the Black male member.

Beat as they take this in.

ADELINE. The Black male what?

HUGO. The phallus.

ADELINE. Phyllis, is she here?

MIFFIE. No, dear, he's talking about. Cocks. Big. Black. Cocks.

The door opens. QM *enters, she wears a shawl.*

Everyone turns and bows, except for LADY ADELINE *who is looking in the wrong direction, and* IAN.

The QM *notices* IAN *and* BILLY, *noticing, gives him a sideways kick on the bum.* IAN *nods his head.*

QM. I do hope I haven't interrupted anything.

HUGO. Not at all, your majesty.

QM. Hugo.

HUGO. Ma'am… Words fail me.

QM. Well, that really would be a first. Are you well?

HUGO. Oh I doubt it, ma'am.

QM. Oh dear.

HUGO. Doesn't it feel a lifetime ago?

QM. What does?

HUGO. Glamis.

QM. Oh I don't think so.

HUGO. It must be, what, fifty years?

QM. Seventy, eighty, one hundred, two hundred and twenty-four, what does it matter? It's just time, isn't it? It doesn't really mean anything.

HUGO. So wise.

She turns to MIFFIE.

QM. Lady Astlebury, you are a waif.

MIFFIE. Her majesty is too kind.

QM. I can barely see you.

MIFFIE. Thank you, ma'am.

QM. You look unnatural.

MIFFIE. You flatter me.

QM. I'm being quite serious. You look unwell, dearie.

MIFFIE. One tries.

QM. Eat! You must eat.

MIFFIE *laughs, semi-hysterical*.

ADELINE. Don't bother, your majesty, I'm told she's a lunatic.

QM. Adeline. How are you?

ADELINE. Well, I'm all right. I'm living with my daughter now.

QM. Which one?

ADELINE. The boring one.

QM. Mary?

ADELINE. Possibly… But it's you I worry about.

QM. Me? Whatever for?

ADELINE *goes towards the* QM, *taking her in her confidence. The* QM *allows it.*

ADELINE. Why aren't we in the palace?

QM. What do you mean?

ADELINE. Has something happened to Bertie?

A silence, as everyone looks at each other.

QM. Yes. Yes, something has happened to Bertie, Adeline dear, but a long time ago.

ADELINE. Did he – ?

QM *is quiet.*

But I just saw him the other day. We had a lovely chat about… Well, I don't remember now but I remember him so clearly. It doesn't make sense.

QM. No, it doesn't. You're quite right. It doesn't make sense at all.

Silence.

(*Changing the tone.*) But here we are.

HUGO. Without drinks.

QM. What's that, Hugo?

HUGO. Nothing, ma'am.

QM. Is that right, Billy? Are they without drinks?

BILLY. No, your majesty. There's tea.

QM. Tea? What is this? The Mad Hatter's Tea Party?

BILLY. It has elements, ma'am.

QM. Oh hello, Jeremy, you're here.

KERR. Ma'am.

QM. Is the funereal tone your doing?

KERR. No, ma'am.

SCENE SIX 87

QM. Then why the long faces and empty glasses?

BILLY. No reason, ma'am.

QM. Time for a change of pace, wouldn't you say then?

KERR. I have no objection, of course, ma'am.

QM. Good. Billy, champagne?

BILLY. Yes, ma'am. Perhaps with dinner?

QM. Perhaps now. What's wrong with you?

BILLY. Sherry?

QM. And the rest.

BILLY. Yes, ma'am.

BILLY goes back towards the central door and knocks it.

FOOTMEN enter, including GWYDION, with wine. They serve the guests through the following:

HUGO. Thank God, I was in very great danger of sobering up.

BILLY lightly pulls or beckons IAN towards him, away from the QM (who clocks it).

QM. Don't thank God, Hugo, thank me.

We see BILLY and IAN whispering but can't hear what they're saying.

HUGO. One and the same, ma'am, one and the same.

QM. You are silly. (*Turning.*) And who is this, Billy?

BILLY. I'm sorry, ma'am. This is Prince... Ian of.

KERR. Lesotho.

QM. Not like you to forget, Billy.

BILLY. I'm sorry, ma'am. A late addition from the palace.

QM. It is a pleasure to meet you, your highness.

The QM does a little curtsy to IAN.

GWYDION drops something again.

GWYDION. Sorry, your majesty.

QM (*to* IAN). Ian, I assume that is an anglicisation of something exotic?

IAN. It's actually pronounced I'n.

QM. Gosh.

BILLY. Gwydion was just telling me that he has news that unfortunately the prince has been called away on urgent family business and will not be able to stay for dinner.

QM. Oh my. Not a revolution I hope. If it is, you'd be better off staying put. They can't seem to get rid of us here. No, I won't have it. I may be a dowager queen but I am still a queen. Surely you can stay?

IAN looks at BILLY.

IAN. If you would like, ma'am.

QM. Hurrah, that's settled. And how are you finding your visit?

IAN. I'm actually from here.

QM. Oh really? Where?

IAN. Tooting.

QM. How clever.

KERR. I thought you were part of the visiting delegation?

BILLY. I think what Prince I'n was meaning is that he spends so much time here he feels like he lives here.

MIFFIE. He's an artist, ma'am.

QM. Ah! That explains everything. Well, you must tell me all about your art.

General hubbub of 'no's.

What's that?

BILLY. It's rather political, ma'am.

MIFFIE. More anatomical I would have said.

SCENE SIX   89

IAN. There is actually something I would like to talk to you about, ma'am.

QM. Yes, please.

IAN. Southall.

QM. Oh did you like it? We recently had it repainted. Well, I say recently – I think it was sixty-eight, was it, Billy?

IAN. Southhall, in London.

QM. Oh.

BILLY. Not too far from Brentford, ma'am.

QM. Well, yes I know it very well. In fact I was just there!

IAN. Do you know about the riots there last week?

QM. Actually I did read something about that.

BILLY. We brought through the 'objets', ma'am.

QM. What 'objets', Billy? Oh yes, Billy does this rather marvellous thing. He finds funny little objects from the royal archive and we all talk about them and it's very jolly.

BILLY *turns and gestures to* GWYDION*'s tray and the* FOOTMAN *to pick up the boxes, now nicely wrapped with name tags.*

MIFFIE. Goodie bags?

QM. No, Miffie dear. You can't keep them. (*To* BILLY.) Make sure she doesn't run off with them, Billy.

IAN. It was an anti-racism protest.

QM. Yes, of course. Terrible business.

IAN. What was?

BILLY. They each have tags.

MIFFIE. Oh I adore it. I'll treasure it always.

QM. No, Miffie dear, you can't keep them. Billy, I'm wondering if wrapping them was necessarily a good idea –

MIFFIE. Thank you so much, ma'am.

QM (*to* BILLY). Make sure to frisk that one.

BILLY. Yes, ma'am.

IAN. A man died.

MIFFIE. Who died? What's going on?

IAN. A protester in Southall.

KERR. Steady on.

MIFFIE. Gosh, I love it. What is it?

She holds up the wheel of an angling rod.

QM. Oh, yes, what is that?

BILLY. It is a reel from an angling rod belonging to your father, your majesty.

QM. Billy, how exactly is that suitable for Miffie?

BILLY. Yes, I wonder if perhaps there's been…

QM. Yes.

IAN. He was killed by a blow to the back of the skull.

MIFFIE. Who? Her father?

IAN. The protester.

ADELINE. What on earth is going on?

HUGO. I appear to have a leaflet about hats.

BILLY. Lady Astlebury's grandmother in a hat. It's from *Tatler*, I believe.

MIFFIE. Oh let's swap.

BILLY. If you'll just wait a moment.

MIFFIE (*referring to* IAN*'s box, which she grabs off him*). What's in this?

She lifts out a card from a box.

Ooopsie something came out.

BILLY. Careful, it's delicate.

QM. What's that.

BILLY. A pressed flower from your coming out. It was intended for Lady Adeline. I'm so sorry, ma'am. They appear to have got muddled.

IAN. The protester was killed by the police.

KERR. Steady on.

IAN. Truncheoned from behind.

KERR. Impossible. If the police needed to use force, then it must have been justified.

IAN. He was hit from behind. The point is, your majesty: this is happening here. In your country and nothing, nothing is being done about it.

KERR. It is not for you to tell her majesty what the point is. And what's happened to your accent?

ADELINE. I say, what's this?

ADELINE holds up the dildo sculpture. BILLY, diving, snatches it from her before the other characters can see it.

QM. Careful, Billy. What's that?

BILLY. A mix-up.

QM. Clearly. Is it for Prince I'n?

BILLY. No, your majesty.

QM. Well, it must be, everyone's been accounted for, I think. Let's see it.

BILLY. Really, your majesty, there has been the most unfortunate but easily fixed mistake. I will just go out and find the correct item.

QM. Yes but what's this item?

BILLY doesn't say anything.

Give it to me.

BILLY *reluctantly pulls his arm from behind his back and passes the dildo to her majesty. She holds it up, considers it from a few angles.*

Are you quite sure this is from our collection?

IAN. It's mine, I made it. (*Quietly, laughingly.*) It's called Black Dawn and it's coming to fuck you all.

Blackout.

Scene Seven

Same location. The Garden Room. Clarence House. An hour later. KERR *and* QM *on their own.*

KERR. He's a prostitute, ma'am.

QM. The prince?

KERR. He is not a prince, ma'am.

QM. No. Yes, I do understand. It is just rather a lot to take in. What will happen to him?

KERR. He's with security.

QM. Yes, well. Good.

KERR. But of course he didn't enter unlawfully. We will look into his record though, see if there's something.

QM. How did he enter?

KERR. Billy, ma'am.

QM. Are we sure?

KERR. Yes, ma'am. Although the prince – the prostitute – is refusing to speak. I understand from a junior but reliable footman, that Billy entertained him here just the other night. Then he returned today and told security that he is Billy's cousin.

QM. Ah, well, that is somewhat different, if he's Billy's relation. One can't choose one's family after all.

KERR. But I'm afraid that story that doesn't quite add up.

QM. Why not?

KERR. Because of the position…

QM. The position?

KERR. Or should I say the state?

QM. I don't know, should you?

KERR. I think it is unlikely they were related.

QM. Because?

KERR is silent.

Jeremy, can you hear me?

KERR. Yes, ma'am.

QM. Am I a queen?

KERR. You are. But it is delicate. I'm sure her majesty can imagine the details.

QM. No, I cannot. Or very rarely. I prefer the facts stated aloud.

KERR. Billy was discovered yesterday… romancing… in the Garden Room.

QM. Romancing?

KERR. Ma'am, I think you know what I speak of.

QM. Do you…? That seems very presumptuous of you. Tell me what happened.

KERR. Billy was seen courting the young man here in the Garden Room, yesterday.

QM. Courting. How romantic. Did he bring flowers?

KERR. No, ma'am.

Beat.

It was more graphic than that.

QM. Poetry?

KERR. Sex, ma'am.

QM. That's quite enough of that.

Silence.

She gets up.

In here?

KERR. This was where they were discovered but it's possible they did all sorts in all sorts of rooms.

QM. Are you sure?

KERR. So it seems unlikely they were related.

QM. I think that's the least of it.

KERR. Exactly. It is a question of security. We suspect the boy. The prostitute is a drug addict. Possibly a communist. As I say, we're investigating.

QM. I see. That is serious.

KERR. He could have been dangerous. He could have caused. He still could, in fact, cause us harm.

QM. Yes, I see.

KERR. I'm afraid there is only one thing we can do, ma'am.

QM. Oh really?

KERR. Yes, ma'am... Billy, ma'am.

QM. Are we quite sure?... I have become somewhat used to Billy.

KERR. Yes, ma'am. As I say, it is a matter of security. The palace just won't allow it.

QM. Have they been told?

KERR. Not yet.

QM. Good. Best to avoid having to discuss, well, anything with Lilibet. She is very... good to me.

KERR. And I think perhaps we can avoid that conversation.

QM. Really? That would be preferable.

KERR. I think we can, if we just remove the subject entirely.

QM. Billy?

Beat.

Yes, I see.

KERR. He will be expecting it, ma'am.

QM. Yes. Well, there it is I suppose.

KERR *smiles*.

Beat.

Try not to look too pleased, Jeremy. He was with us a long time.

Beat.

Will you leave us? I need a moment.

KERR. Yes, ma'am.

He leaves.

She is quiet.

She takes off her shawl to reveal a glittering necklace.

Lighting change as we move back in time to 1952 – a few months have passed.

YOUNG BILLY *enters*.

QM. Billy! How wonderful it's you. But what do I do now? I'm wide awake. Didn't want to outstay my welcome so I rushed home. Rushed, rushed as if I was off to some important business of state or a husband. Or a child even. When in fact what I was doing was running away from a party just to sit in this room. Isn't life queer, Billy?

BILLY. I wouldn't know, ma'am.

QM. Well, it is. Twenty years spent at the very point of a knife slashing through history and then here with you. Life is queer. Now what I need to do is take this bloody necklace off. It's like a diamond noose.

BILLY. I'll get one of the maids.

QM. No, you can manage.

BILLY. Are you sure?

QM. I'm always sure.

She bows her neck.

BILLY *gingerly unclasps it and raises it above.*

For a moment they both look at it as it sparkles in the light.

BILLY. It's heavy.

QM. Isn't it?

BILLY. But also, so fine.

QM. It's a Boucheron. Not terribly old but a beauty. A gift from Mrs Greville. She was a little gnome made of money. I was terribly fond of her. Do you know, if I were to insure you, insure your life I mean, it would not come close to its value.

BILLY. Where shall I put it, ma'am?

She stands.

QM. Put it on.

BILLY. Ma'am?

QM. You heard me.

BILLY. I can't.

QM. You can.

BILLY. I mustn't.

QM. That is the correct answer, now put it on. And this.

She takes her diamond tiara and puts it on his head.

Oh yes. What fun. Go take a look.

He looks at himself in a mirror.

Puts on the necklace.

Turn around.

He turns and curtsies.

He strikes some poses copied from society pages.

She laughs.

Yes, I do think perhaps I'm going mad.

And laughs again.

Do you know how to dance?

YOUNG BILLY. Not really, ma'am.

QM. Well, I will teach you and then we will dance. And each night when I have to leave early, or I am not invited, we will carry on the ball. Just you and me. Agreed?

YOUNG BILLY. Agreed.

QM. Wonderful. That way neither of us need be lonely again. Would you like that?

YOUNG BILLY. More than anything, ma'am.

They dance out of the space.

Scene Eight

Back in the present. Clarence House, 1979. Garden Room. Dusk.

BILLY *enters and paces the room. We see* GWYDION *cross past the open door.* BILLY *sees him.*

BILLY. Daff!

Silence.

Dafne…

GWYDION *walks back into view.*

GWYDION. Sorry, sir, I didn't see you.

BILLY. Is that right?

GWYDION. Can I get you anything?

BILLY. What's happening?

GWYDION. I don't know, sir. What did they say?

BILLY. To wait.

GWYDION *keeps quiet.*

Spit it out, boy? What's happening? Who have they spoken to?

GWYDION. The guard house.

BILLY. The three blind mice. They'll get nothing useful out of them. Who else?

GWYDION. People.

BILLY. People? Helpful. Who?

GWYDION. Everyone. The maids, the footmen, the kitchen. They're asking everyone questions.

BILLY. Are they? And what is everyone saying?

GWYDION. I don't know. Different things. Everyone has heard a different thing. Some people are saying the prince killed a goat with a dildo.

BILLY. Good. The more fanciful the better, it's easier to dismiss as gossip. The key thing is for you to keep your mouth shut. All they've got to go on is his word and no one will listen to him. He's clearly stark raving mad and a communist. That was clear to everyone. Kerr will need more than that to get rid of me.

GWYDION. Are you sure?

BILLY. Absolutely. She needs me, you see. That's what Kerr doesn't see. She needs me to be me. Not just to serve the palace blindly and mutely like him but to bend the rules to make sure she is still treated like a queen, do you see?

GWYDION. But then why risk it all?

BILLY. No idea at all. I just did it. I just do it. It's all very odd. Very queer.

GWYDION. But you have a plan though, don't you…?

BILLY. What do you mean?

GWYDION. If they do believe him.

BILLY. She won't.

GWYDION. Or someone talks.

BILLY. Who would talk? Besides, no one knows he was here the other night except me and you.

Pause.

(*Realising.*) Daff?

GWYDION. I'm sorry, sir.

BILLY. Oh Daff.

BILLY *turns his back on* GWYDION *and towards us. He sinks to the ground – a crouch, then a kneel, then a ball. Or some gesture of defeat.*

GWYDION. Please, Billy, don't.

GWYDION *goes to him.*

Please, Billy, get up.

BILLY. –

GWYDION. They threatened the police on me. I didn't know what to say, I didn't say anything bad though, I just said he was your friend. Billy?

BILLY. –

GWYDION. I'm sorry, Billy.

Sighing, BILLY *raises his head.*

BILLY. Dafne?

GWYDION. Yes.

BILLY. Don't ever call me Billy. My name is sir.

GWYDION. Very good, sir.

He gets up, carefully dusts off his knees.

BILLY. Well, shall we get a drink, Dafne?

He moves towards the drinks cabinet.

GWYDION. Are you sure that's a good idea?

BILLY. You'll have a whisky.

GWYDION. I don't like whisky.

BILLY. Neither do I but I don't think I have it in me to do a gin and tonic.

He pours a whisky for them.

GWYDION *goes to sit down on the sofa.*

What are you doing?

GWYDION. Sitting down.

BILLY. Not allowed, as you know.

GWYDION. I know but I think –

BILLY. The job is to stand.

GWYDION. I don't understand you, Billy.

BILLY. The rules are the rules.

He hands the drink to GWYDION. *They stand and clink glasses.*

GWYDION. I really am sorry. I panicked.

BILLY. Too late for all that.

GWYDION. What will you do now? You're still young, you could do anything.

BILLY. Am I? Old dogs and all that.

GWYDION. Perhaps you're not happy here, Billy?

BILLY. Happy? No I never asked to be happy. That is for your generation. But I suppose, yes, sometimes I do think, sometimes I do wonder when I am standing and waiting by her side, hours at a time sometimes, my feet and back aching to the point of breaking, sometimes I do wonder... why? Why? What's going to happen? Nothing's going to change. Which, of course, is the point. That's the point of all of this. Nothing must change; I have stopped time for her. I have fashioned a court out of leftovers and cast-offs and found glamour where I can in the margins.

Beat.

Marginalia, darling, that's all I am – but sometimes.

Beat.

Sometimes, the ache in the feet, the ache in the back, you know, the ache in the soul... But that is for another life perhaps.

Beat.

Enough. What's the time?

GWYDION. Walkies.

BILLY. I tell you what I won't miss? Those fucking dogs. Those fucking shitting dogs.

GWYDION *laughs.*

She once charted a private jet, a private jet just me and a corgi named Hazel, an entire plane to ourselves because her majesty worried she'd be lonely in town. Hazel, not her majesty. Although she does get terribly lonely, of course. Terribly lonely.

He drinks.

GWYDION. It's not so bad out there, Billy, you know.

BILLY. What isn't?

GWYDION. Real life.

BILLY. Perhaps.

GWYDION. I think you might like it.

KERR enters.

KERR. Billy.

BILLY. Kerr.

KERR. Her majesty will be in presently. She would like to speak to you.

BILLY. Of course. I will make sure the tea is ready.

KERR. Very good. And Billy?

BILLY. Yes, sir.

KERR. Goodbye and good riddance.

BILLY. Mr Kerr?

BILLY goes up to KERR, pulls him close and gives him a big snog.

KERR (*pulling away*). Billy!

BILLY. Don't fight it. Au revoir, Mr Kerr.

He exits with a flourish. Embarrassed, KERR starts to hurry across the space.

GWYDION (*to* KERR). Sir?

KERR. Yes, Gwydion. What is it?

GWYDION. I want to leave.

KERR. Now? Your shift's barely started.

GWYDION. I want to leave Clarence House.

KERR. Whatever for?

GWYDION. I don't think this is for me.

KERR. What about what we discussed? A position with the Prince of Wales.

GWYDION. I'm not interested.

KERR. Now is not a good time. Can you not wait?

GWYDION. No, sir. I can't. I have to get out of here.

KERR. Gwydion!

GWYDION exits, followed by KERR.

The QM *enters. She goes back to the window and sits down.*

She looks around for something. Can't find it. Stands up again.

QM. Billy?

BILLY *enters, followed by a corgi who runs towards the* QM.

BILLY. Yes, ma'am.

QM. My reading glasses.

BILLY. Yes, ma'am.

He goes to a spot and finds them; he brings them back.

QM. Very good.

BILLY. Would her majesty like her magazine?

QM. No.

Beat.

Yes.

He hands her the magazine.

Thank you, Billy.

Beat.

Billy, would you like to sit down?

BILLY. Ma'am?

QM (*off his reaction*). What's wrong? There if you like.

BILLY. No, ma'am. A footman stands. A footman waits.

QM. Yes, I suppose you all do, don't you? I hadn't thought of it. I wonder though is there nothing else you want to do? You do rather enjoy the spotlight. I have often wondered if you would prefer the stage.

BILLY. Me? Heavens, no. Can you imagine?

QM (*dryly*). I can actually.

BILLY. I'm a little too old for that, ma'am.

QM. Hardly, you're a boy.

BILLY. Her majesty is too kind.

QM. Heavens, if you're old what does that make me? Don't answer that of course.

BILLY. Of course.

QM. I wonder though if you are happy here.

BILLY. How can you ask that, ma'am?

QM. Because you keep being naughty.

BILLY. Yes, I can be a bit of a silly, ma'am.

QM (*harder*). Rather more than that, Billy. You have made a mess for yourself. And me.

BILLY. Ma'am, I never intended to.

QM. I have no interest in the details, you understand.

BILLY. Yes, ma'am.

SCENE EIGHT   105

QM. I have been extraordinarily tolerant I believe. There are many of my generation who are considerably less so I believe, but I have no quarrel with people like you. Noël as you know was a great friend. I accept that there are many who are not the marrying kind. But I believe in society everyone must have a place, so why shouldn't you? Why shouldn't you be useful? After all, without a family you have so much more time, which I must assume is why there are so many of you in service. And of course, you do all seem to be so terribly creative and entertaining and that is something of a boon. You have been a boon to me in trying times, there's no denying it but –

BILLY. Ma'am.

QM. Let me finish, Billy, this is hard for me.

BILLY. Yes, ma'am.

QM. All I have asked. All I have ever asked is loyalty.

BILLY. Yes, ma'am. And you can count on my loyalty until the day I die.

QM. Well.

BILLY. And my discretion.

QM. Is that right?

BILLY. Yes, ma'am.

QM. But you haven't been discreet.

BILLY. I have never spoken a word of anything I have ever seen or heard in this house, ma'am. And I never will.

She stands, troubled, and puts down the dog.

QM. Billy, are you being clever?

BILLY. Ma'am?

QM. Because we can't have that. Are you, what's the word? Insinuating something by referring to intimacies?

BILLY. Absolutely not.

QM. Because I would remind you that we are very stupid creatures, you and I.

BILLY. Yes, ma'am.

QM. We don't have the capacity for all of that.

BILLY. Yes, ma'am.

QM. We are very stupid creatures but we know our place, is that not right? You and I?

Beat.

Or at least that's what I always felt but perhaps I have misjudged you.

He goes down on his knees.

BILLY. Forgive me.

QM. Oh dear no please. No scenes.

BILLY. If you'll just let me speak.

QM. No.

BILLY. Please. There is nothing I wouldn't do.

Beat.

QM. Hazel.

BILLY. Ma'am?

QM. Hazel has had an accident.

BILLY *sees the dog and a large turd which has now appeared near it.*

BILLY. Yes, ma'am. It happens.

QM. Yes it does.

BILLY. I'll get a maid.

QM. No, Billy. You do it.

BILLY. Of course.

He starts to stand.

Let me just get my gloves.

QM. No time for that, it's staining the rug. Pick it up.

BILLY *looks at* QM. *This is a test. Will he accept?*

Or perhaps young Gwydion will do it?

BILLY *gets back down on his knees, he slowly, too slowly, picks up the shit with his hands.*

Poor Hazel.

BILLY. Yes, ma'am.

He starts to stand.

QM. Careful, Billy. You've got some on your shoe. Get off the carpet, Billy!

He goes back down so he is almost dog-like on all fours, apart from the shit which he holds in one hand, outstretched so that it won't fall.

He starts to crawl, three-legged, to the door.

Hazel would be terribly embarrassed.

He tries to move faster, she walks behind him, almost like she is walking a dog.

Quick. Quick. Quicker.

He starts barking and scampering around the room.

Down, boy, down.

He calms down.

Good boy.

She strokes his head.

Now get rid of that and come back here.

He runs, still dog-like, out of the room.

Beat.

The QM *sits calmly.*

He re-enters, upright but frazzled.

BILLY. Ma'am?

QM. Yes, Billy.

BILLY. Is there anything else, ma'am?

QM. No, I think we have all we need, now. Don't you?

BILLY. Yes, ma'am.

BILLY goes to the drinks cabinet and starts making her a drink. We see his shoulders sag as the stage goes dark around them.

Scene Nine

Same location. BILLY *still in the centre as* FOOTMEN *or* MAIDS *enter carrying flowers in vases. It is a conscious echo of the first scene.*

They wait for him to give orders.

He raises his head and begins, his confidence returning as he goes on.

BILLY. Rosewood.

One moves towards a rosewood cabinet, keeping to the side of the space.

Occasional.

Another one peels off towards the occasional table.

Sideboard.

Another one goes towards a sideboard.

Plinth. Plinth.

One goes towards a plinth. Together the FOOTMEN *lay the flowers down in sync for his consideration. They wait for his approval.*

YOUNG BILLY *enters, he looks at his older self.*

YOUNG BILLY. I stayed with the Queen Mother for a further twenty-three years.

When she died in 2002, I was (finally) retired and forced to move out of Clarence House, where I had worked and lived for nearly fifty years.

For the next five years I lived alone in a flat in Kennington, South London. I died on 23 November 2007, aged seventy-two.

My funeral took place at St James's Palace… in the Queen's Chapel.

BILLY *looks at* YOUNG BILLY. *A moment of mutual recognition. He turns and surveys the room, and then turns to the audience.*

BILLY. Yes, there it is. Just so.

End.

MGC

MGC is a London-based company that produces work across all media, nationally and internationally. MGC also provides a General Management service to other producers and looks after a select group of creative practitioners.

MGC recent productions include: *Orlando* with Emma Corrin (West End), *Dawn French is a Huge Tw*t* (UK tour), and *The Lemon Table* with Ian McDiarmid (UK tour). Other productions include: In the West End, *The Lieutenant of Inishmore* with Aidan Turner, *Red* with Alfred Molina and Alfred Enoch, *Labour of Love* (co-produced with Headlong) with Martin Freeman and Tamsin Greig, *Photograph 51* with Nicole Kidman, *Henry V* with Jude Law, *A Midsummer Night's Dream* with David Walliams and Sheridan Smith, *The Cripple of Inishmaan* with Daniel Radcliffe (and on Broadway), *Peter and Alice* with Judi Dench and Ben Whishaw, *Privates on Parade* with Simon Russell Beale, and *Hughie* on Broadway with Forest Whitaker. MGC co-produced (with Emily Dobbs Productions) *The Dazzle* with Andrew Scott, and Dawn French's *30 Million Minutes* (with Phil McIntyre Entertainment) in the West End, and on tour in the UK and internationally.

Films include: *My Policeman* (2022) starring Harry Styles, Emma Corrin, Gina McKee, Linus Roache, David Dawson and Rupert Everett, and *Genius* (2016) starring Colin Firth, Jude Law, Nicole Kidman, and Laura Linney.

MichaelGrandageCompany.com

www.nickhernbooks.co.uk

facebook.com/nickhernbooks

twitter.com/nickhernbooks